The Eleventh Commandment

The Next Step in Social Spiritual Development

A New Code to Bring Humanity
To a Higher Level of Spiritual Awareness

By
Stephen Knapp

COVER PHOTO: A small hilltop temple pointing to the heavens to better intercept the higher awareness that is waiting to be received. Taken in Leh, India by Stephen Knapp.

ISBN-10: 198601004X
ISBN-13: 978-1986010047

Published by
The World Relief Network,
Detroit, Michigan

You can find out more about Stephen Knapp and his books, free ebooks, research, and numerous articles and photos, along with many other spiritual resources at:

www.Stephen-Knapp.com
http://stephenknapp.info
http://stephenknapp.wordpress.com

Other books by the author:

1. The Secret Teachings of the Vedas: The Eastern Answers to the Mysteries of Life
2. The Universal Path to Enlightenment
3. The Vedic Prophecies: A New Look into the Future
4. How the Universe was Created and Our Purpose In It
5. Toward World Peace: Seeing the Unity Between Us All
6. Facing Death: Welcoming the Afterlife
7. The Key to Real Happiness
8. Proof of Vedic Culture's Global Existence
9. The Heart of Hinduism: The Eastern Path to Freedom, Enlightenment and Illumination
10. The Power of the Dharma: An Introduction to Hinduism and Vedic Culture
11. Vedic Culture: The Difference it can Make in Your Life
12. Reincarnation & Karma: How They Really Affect Us
13. The Eleventh Commandment: The Next Step for Social Spiritual Development
14. Seeing Spiritual India: A Guide to Temples, Holy Sites, Festivals and Traditions
15. Crimes Against India: And the Need to Protect its Ancient Vedic Tradition
16. Destined for Infinity, a spiritual adventure in the Himalayas
17. Yoga and Meditation: Their Real Purpose and How to Get Started
18. Avatars, Gods and Goddesses of Vedic Culture: Understanding the Characteristics, Powers and Positions of the Hindu Divinities
19. The Soul: Understanding Our Real Identity
20. Prayers, Mantras and Gayatris: A Collection for Insights, Protection, Spiritual Growth, and Many Other Blessings
21. Krishna Deities and Their Miracles: How the Images of Lord Krishna Interact with Their Devotees.
22. Defending Vedic Dharma: Tackling the Issues to Make a Difference.
23. Advancements of Ancient India's Vedic Culture.
24. Spreading Vedic Traditions Through Temples.
25. The Bhakti-yoga Handbook: A Guide to Beginning the Essentials of Devotional Yoga
26. Lord Krishna and His Essential Teachings
27. Mysteries of the Ancient Vedic Empire.
28. Casteism in India
29. Ancient History of Vedic Culture
30. A Complete Review of Vedic Literature
31. Bhakti-Yoga: The Easy Path of Devotional Yoga

CONTENTS

Chapter One: 3
The Search for Fulfillment

Chapter Two: 11
The Eleventh Commandment
      The Great Recognition * The Great Realization * Curing
      the Global Crisis

Chapter Three: 26
Identifying the Higher Self

Chapter Four: 33
Recognizing the Divine Within Yourself

Chapter Five: 35
Seeing the Divine All Around You

Chapter Six: 38
Seeing Our Inner Unity

Chapter Seven: 45
Opening Our Hearts to One Another

Chapter Eight: 53
Utilizing Higher Consciousness in Everyday Life

Chapter Nine: 58
Identifying Our False Self

Chapter Ten: 66
Finding Contentment and Joy

Chapter Eleven: 70
Politics and Leadership According to the 11th Commandment

Chapter Twelve: 77
Economics According to the 11th Commandment

Chapter Thirteen: 83
Nonviolence According to the 11th Commandment

Chapter Fourteen: 88
Diet According to the 11th Commandment

Chapter Fifteen: 94
Environmentalism According to the 11th Commandment

Chapter Sixteen: 98
Being Aware of Reactions to Our Activities and Intentions

Chapter Seventeen: 100
Being a Reflection of God's Unconditional Love

Chapter Eighteen: 107
Manifesting God's Plan for Humanity and the World

Chapter Nineteen: 111
Social Change to Manifest a New Paradigm

Chapter Twenty: 115
Open Up to the Great Life Within

Conclusion: 120
Giving the 11th Commandment to Others

Index   124

About the Author   127

CHAPTER ONE

The Search for Fulfillment

      Society has been evolving for many years, progressing to the degree that its particular knowledge, understanding, and perception allow. Many people are ready and anticipating the next step in the spiritual progress of the planet that could uplift the whole society and bring a new level of peace and understanding to the world. From the various religions of the world, we have acquired certain spiritual codes and rules that we have chosen to live by, and that we have used as tools to guide us, and they have served us well. However, most would agree that there is a need to enhance humanity's progress, even if it takes new insights and principles to add to what we already have, or even to supersede those codes that no longer provide the necessary clarity for a sharper spiritual perception and more refined awareness. Thus, this new code expects us to sophisticate ourselves to a higher level of civility, to a new dimension of activity, and to adopt progressive changes beyond what we had followed in the past. But it must be understood that its purpose is to assist us in acquiring a higher degree of spiritual perception and personal realization and development.

      Herein is the next step for consideration, which can be used as a tool for guidance, and for setting a higher standard in our society today. This can be used by anyone from any background or culture, and easily suites an interfaith dialog to propel humanity at large toward a closer spiritual unity with each other and with God. With this new principle, we can easily instill within our social structure a mutual respect for one another and a universal understanding of what we are and the spiritual similarities that we all share. The new realizations and vision that we need to attain, in order to achieve this goal, will then become apparent to us.

This new commandment expects and directs us toward a change in our social awareness and spiritual consciousness. It is conceived, formulated, and now provided to assist humanity in reaching its true destiny, and to bring a new spiritual dimension into the basic fabric of our ordinary, every day life. It is a key that unlocks the doors of perception, and opens up a whole new aspect of spiritual understanding for all of us to view. It is the commandment which precepts us to gain the knowledge of the hidden mysteries, which have for so long remained an enigma to the confused and misdirected men of this world. It holds the key which unlocks the answers to man's quest for peace and happiness, and the next step for spiritual growth on a dynamic and all-inclusive social level.

Everyone in the world wants a safe, secure, and happy life. Everyone wants to have a fulfilling existence while living in peace and cooperation with their loved ones. Everyone wants to live life directed towards a purpose: feeling as though they are a part of something bigger than themselves, guided with intention and clarity, and striving for a promised destiny, or at least a positive future.

However, when the challenges of life seem overwhelming, everyone at some time wants to feel that there is still a level or a dimension where everything is balanced, harmonious, and makes sense. No matter what may happen, or how confusing things seem to be, they would like to experience that feeling of being fixed and focused, unaffected by their external circumstances. In their deepest thoughts, many people want to feel that they have a rightful place for themselves in the Universal Presence and love that can be found everywhere, if only we can recognize it and be open to it.

When people can experience even a small glimpse of that awareness, they will also perceive that they are a part of a Universal Presence, or God, and a part of the ever-loving light that accepts them unconditionally. This provides an incredible relief to the complexities of life that most people endure. By opening up to this higher vision, people will see that they are indeed a part of

God, and that God is a part of them, and that nothing will ever alter that relationship. It only needs to be more fully developed.

The key is found in removing the ignorance or darkness that keeps so many of us from perceiving that reality. Once a person encounters this spiritual truth, life will no longer be a mystery for them to solve, or a question to ponder, but then life becomes a wonderful reality to experience. It becomes an adventure in which untold possibilities open up to us. It becomes a joy in which we are eager to participate. Then life as we know it in this restricted, three-dimensional existence becomes another aspect of the unlimited spiritual strata that is natural to the soul. It becomes another aspect of seeing the inner similarities between all of us and, indeed, among all life. We can then see how we are all connected. What I do affects you and what you do affects me, and influences the whole planet to whatever degree our actions spread in our sphere of activity, either positive or negative. With such a perception, based on inner spiritual awareness, this world becomes a far different place than before. Then you will find that the more people you meet who can share this perception, the more the spiritual dimension can be revealed and manifest on this earthly plane. Then the troubles that seem so common between countries, cultures, and races of people will become increasingly antiquated, outgrown, and unnecessary, and the more people will turn to better solutions. It is time for a last chance at reaching this perception for society as a whole. In other words, we are running out of time for this reality to manifest in the consciousness of society at large. It is time for society to reach this awareness on a wide scale in order for it to take the next step in social spiritual development. That is the reason why this 11th commandment is being presented.

Understanding and practicing this 11th commandment will more strongly connect everyone to the omnipresent spiritual reality known as the Supreme Creator. It will increase our insight into our relationship with this lofty spiritual dimension, and it will heighten our sense of purpose and fulfillment in a natural way. The more people who strive for this elevated consciousness, the more the vibrational level of the whole planet will rise to a higher frequency, a higher level of creating a positive future in which everyone can benefit.

This will assist people all over the world to attain a higher state of awareness and perception. It will certainly lead to a greater level of global peace and cooperation, as well as individual fulfillment. There is no greater need in the world today.

The duty of God towards humanity is to supply that knowledge by which society may gain clarity of who and what they are, and gain freedom from the darkness of egoism or bodily consciousness. This also includes providing the world with those elevated individuals who can relate such spiritual information to society. This knowledge, being referred to as that which belongs to the universal spiritual truths, is eternal and applicable to everyone, and can be applied anywhere and in anyone's status of life. This knowledge, being eternal, will circulate throughout the creation in many ways, and in many forms. It will be regularly found at the right time, by the right people, and for the right cause. It will assist humanity in conquering the innumerable misunderstandings they have: such as ignorance of themselves, of who they are, of God, and of the purpose of life. When the accurate and genuine nature of this knowledge is presented, without being tinged by humanity's own limited perception of themselves and the Absolute Truth, it will also instill a rise in consciousness and insight in those who accept it as the solution to establishing genuine peace in the world. It will bring down the barriers of the self-inflicted limitations, which thus cause the quarrels and wars that presently fill the world in this age, and which are all so unnecessary. The duty of humanity is to take this knowledge seriously. We are often not determined enough about learning, growing, and changing ourselves in such a way in order to help change the world.

People must not only hear of the Truth, they also must live in a style by which their consciousness changes so they can see the Truth. In other words, we must act in ways to purify our consciousness and raise our perception to see the higher levels of spiritual reality that not only exist all around us, but in which we are a part. It is not enough to merely have faith. In this way, everyone is encouraged to undertake the path that leads to the great realization. The great realization is to first understand, and then later to perceive by direct experience, one's true spiritual identity. This true identity that is presently within us, but nonetheless beyond the physical body, is our real self. This experience and perception can be attained by genuine spiritual development. It can then be shared with all others without force, without conversion tactics, but in a natural way of growth and maturity.

It is called the great realization because of the depth of perception that can be attained when one achieves it, and also because of the number of people that are meant to attain it. Thus, the ultimate spiritual path is that which provides inward and individual development and is not mere dogma that is institutionally forced on others. Philosophies or religions that are forced often breed fanaticism, and any great realization is not to be found in fanaticism. Extremism, in any form, is only a sign of great immaturity. Implementing and understanding this 11th commandment will assure that anyone of any tradition will rise to the next step in widespread social spiritual development.

We must understand that what we often call religion should be a means to assist us in our search for the Absolute Truth, or God. It should be a way of asking the questions, and receiving the answers that we need in order for us to understand certain higher realities. It should not be something that is merely accepted blindly, or something that once realized causes us to stop searching anymore for anything at all. We should not stop our continued spiritual progress. Otherwise, religion becomes an external authority that dictates our thoughts and actions, rather than a means to provide real spiritual awareness and maturity that guides us in the proper direction and to the natural insights and answers. If it is merely a belief system, then religion becomes an exclusivist idea that proposes that all those who do not believe in the way that we do are inferior to us, and therefore must be converted to our way of thinking. This leads to misunderstanding and conflicts of all kinds. It focuses our purposes on how to eliminate the non-believers, rather than helping people find genuine union with God, thus raising the consciousness of all. This does not bring us toward being better people, it only brings out the dogma which inflicts people with the idea that everyone else must change and accept their particular religion. When so many people feel this way, the world remains a place of chaos and disunity.

The more that people can see the backward nature of this dogmatic line of thinking, which is often bereft of genuine spiritual perception, the more that we will see a decline in religious fundamentalism. Religion must be based on universal spiritual truth, the truth that is applicable to everyone, regardless of bodily distinctions, cultural differences, or location. It should not be based on mere opinion, and the ever-changing conventions of humanity. Freedom of religious expression, based on love of God, or the search for truth, is natural. We are all intelligent beings on the road to self-discovery. We are not animals herded into one particular way of spiritual inquiry. This will only stifle the development of our deeper consciousness. We are meant to grow and blossom in our realizations of our connection with the Divine within us. God is not separate from us, and there are many ways to discover this, for which we must have the freedom to engage in this quest. Without this freedom, humanity will never reach its full potential, since this quest is an ever-present part of humanity's character and disposition.

In our search for fulfillment, we must know that real happiness comes from the Divine. It comes from two ways: being on the path to reach the Divine, or from contact with the Divine. We may presently have so much material facility, whether it is a big house, a fancy car, or many electronic appliances and gadgets, etc. But, look at how many people are still crying for more, or are worried about how to maintain and not lose what they have, or so many other problems that are but superficial to our real identity as a spiritual being. Where is the contentment in any of this? Where is the fulfillment in these fleeting pleasures? The path of materialism cannot provide complete fulfillment, and often gives only momentary feelings of pleasure while creating what often becomes increasingly numerous problems and aggravations.

The knowledge that you are reading is nothing new. It existed before the universal creation, and it will continue to exist within the spiritual frequencies that will outlast the material worlds. It shows the way to bring in that spiritual vibration to these material planets and change the consciousness of society. But, it only occurs if people lose their pride and realize the futility of relying on what is nothing more than their own misgivings, which exist in the dictates of the mind and senses. One must go to a higher source of guidance and intelligence, which is the purpose of real spiritual knowledge.

By understanding our own true spiritual identity, which basically identifies us as not being this body but the soul within, then our aim of life can entirely change. We can be free from all the wants, demands, and desires it takes to satisfy our mind and senses, and we can direct ourselves in the proper way so that we can be at peace, fully content, and even blissful.

You must know peace in your heart before you can be a true peacemaker for the world. When you are established in peace, your heart becomes a temple of the Divine, and then you can see all others as parts of the Divine. Then, you can be a true friend to everyone in the world. When there is such a vision and mindset in an increasing number of people, peace can spread over the whole planet.

No matter how much wealth we have, no matter how much money we earn, no matter how many possessions we keep, or how opulent our homes may be, none of these can give us true peace. Without peace, there is no real happiness, but only fleeting moments of pleasure which reside in those instances of forgetfulness of our problems, beginning with such issues as old age, disease and death. Without peace, even if you own or control a whole kingdom, your life may still feel empty. So, no matter what you have, all that is on the material and bodily level of existence is taken away at the time of death, at the end of your short life. Then, what will happen? If you are not prepared for what lies beyond death, then you will have wasted your valuable human life on shallow goals. No one should be this foolish as to waste his or her existence on mere materialistic pursuits. Everyone should make spiritual progress, which is the goal of life, and attain self-realization, peace and contentment. You can only have true contentment if you have control over your mind and senses, and utilize the proper focus and intent. This is the way toward real fulfillment, both individually and collectively, in reaching the goal of life.

This spiritual knowledge can change the world by changing those who want to perceive this truth. However, it may also be viewed as the enemy of those who wish to keep the general masses of people in the darkness of ignorance for their own purposes. There are people who want ignorance to prevail for their own profits or control. For that reason, many are those who will view this knowledge as something that should be kept secret, or forbidden, or even outlawed.

Many are those who would view this knowledge as the ultimate revolution, the ultimate giver of freedom, or the ultimate demise of their own evil agenda, if that is what they have in mind. A spiritual revolution must begin in order to allow everyone to become more spiritually alive and aware. It must be a global transformation, though it may start on an individual basis.

This knowledge is now being presented through the invocation of those with higher perception, and who have purified minds and consciousness. This knowledge is for the continued evolutionary development of all beings within the confines of this limited and temporary material creation. If you now hold this in your hands, it is not a mere accident of fate. It is now a tool to assist you in fulfilling the higher purposes of your existence, even the higher destiny of all living beings in this world.

CHAPTER TWO

The Eleventh Commandment

As we approach a new era of development, albeit a new level of understanding, we are also given a new code for guidance. This new spiritual understanding is actually old knowledge, but more relevant today than ever before. If we are to work together, we must reach a united level of spiritual progress and perception for mutual regard and respect. Presently, this 11th commandment can provide a premier form of assistance that we can all focus on, and from which we can move forward with a similar consciousness.

This commandment centralizes and focuses for us the next step in our social spiritual development. It goes beyond basic moral codes, yet all moral principles are but outgrowths of this simple, deep commandment. Its depth is that it does not require everyone to merely follow a new rule superficially, but it prompts everyone to go within themselves, to actually transform one's consciousness and understanding of themselves and others in a progressive way. It expects you to change the way you view life, and the way you interact with all other beings. It expects that you come closer to opening the door to the spiritual dimension available to you. It behooves you to see how close you are to bringing that dimension into your life and, indeed, throughout the world. It should be followed so that you do not get mislead or confused by other codes that are less than harmonious, or less than able to hold or be based on the eternal, spiritual truths. This 11th commandment is:

"Thou shall recognize the Divinity in all living beings, and that the spirit in all life is part of the Supreme Spirit."

As we have said, this may sound like an old standard, and is, therefore, easy enough to follow. However, even a child of eight may understand this principle, but it is seen that hardly a man of eighty has put it into real practice, perceiving the actual depths to which it refers. Now the time has come: If the planetary civilization is going to move forward, humanity must seriously contemplate this commandment on all levels. Therefore, the meaning of this commandment and how the deeper realization of it will affect all levels of life needs to be explained more thoroughly, which will be provided throughout the rest of the book.

Any human beings who have their hearts open towards God, and are freed from ignorance, will easily see the common sense and logic of implementing this 11th commandment. This commandment will bring about a new paradigm for the world, if everyone would follow it as best they can. It does not depend on an artificial, outward show, but it depends on the inner and permanent realizations that propel one's consciousness to higher levels of perceiving the universal spiritual truths. Individual change must come from within. The real treasure that each person seeks is to be found within. Those who are mature in spiritual understanding will know this. Those who are not so experienced must persevere with faith and know that glimpses of the truth are not so far away. The more you put into the spiritual path, the more it will give back to you.

How can the plan of God manifest within you if you are not truly developed in spiritual understanding? How can humanity bring the light of spiritual knowledge forthwith into society if their hearts are closed to God, and closed to recognizing the Divine in each living being? This must go beyond mere faith in words or a doctrine. Mere faith or belief is not enough. Those who are intelligent will know that practical spiritual knowledge must be realized and applied. The energy and parts of God surround us, but our ignorance and attachment to matter makes us blind to this practical truth. Furthermore, some aspects of the paths that we call religions simply encourage such blindness. Religion based on locality, race, ethnicity, or caste will deter genuine progress for humanity, not promote it. It will keep us bound up in seeing distinctions of material forms rather than the spiritual reality that exists within them. From such darkness, divisions are created, leaving the potential for unity and cooperation far behind. From such darkness or ignorance, mutual respect and consideration toward all living beings will be lost. From such darkness, cruelty will grow, making room for hatred, which can then escalate to war and the insanity that follows. This has already happened many times. This madness of anger can sometimes last for generations, thus ruining society's potential for higher spiritual growth, which is curbed like a glass ceiling keeping us from reaching new heights.

You who are absorbed in such bitterness or dislike of beings that are different from you create a dark future for society and the planet, and a darker future for yourselves. You bring the backwardness of such consciousness into the field of activity on Earth and turn its bright existence into a world of difficulties, unrest, dissatisfaction, and quarrel. You turn it into a hellish place. You may think you are bringing the world toward your conception of God by your dogmatic reasoning, but you are fooled by your own rhetoric. You are blinded by your faulty ideas of what God wants.

It must be noted that the lack of unity and harmony in the world begins in our own minds and in our own consciousness. This is the original source of pollution and corruption. This creates the divisiveness which is unnatural. From the misunderstanding of whom, and of what we are, we create and follow the wrong aim of life. From selfish materialistic endeavors, which at first may seem like new conveniences, come harsh reversals. From greedily using up all our resources, come the shortages that follow. From this aim of life, acting according to our false nature for material happiness and sensual pleasure, comes what is referred to as sin that manifests as difficulties. This can all be corrected by adjusting our consciousness and vision with the spiritual knowledge indicated in this 11th commandment.

Attachment to our material form, which is made of temporary matter, creates our basic misunderstanding of who we are, and of the proper goals of life. Harmony can only manifest when we are in tune with what brings harmony and balance, and that is the spiritual stratum, our real identity. We may look for happiness outside of ourselves, through our senses, but real happiness starts from within. There you will find the doorway that can lead to the greatest bliss in union with God. Do not be lead astray. Be determined to find this door on the path to real freedom, in spite of the changing nature of your material surroundings.

When we understand ourselves as beings of light and we start to bring that inner life into our outer existence, then light, wisdom, unity, cooperation, and joy can abound for all. It will also affect those around us in our sphere of activity, no matter how big or small it is. This is what will help create a positive world, which will manifest an increasingly uplifting future. A people without proper direction, or who are ignorant of the inner light and unable to let it shine forth, live in a world of darkness, not only for themselves but also for others. What kind of a world do you want to live in? The perfect knowledge to help you with this decision is being given to you. Your future is up to you. It is your choice to make the difference.

Henceforth, choose your association and friends carefully. Take up friendship with those of the light, if you want to invoke your own lightness of being. One who is of the light can brighten others. The more we understand our inner spiritual identity, which is eternal and full of knowledge and bliss, the more we will open ourselves to our full potential. Beware of those in darkness less they catch you like a whirlpool, taking you to the depths of despair, fear and confusion. When you are ready, become one of the light to bring brightness to others and free the world of fear and ruination. Then, join together with others who are like-minded, for to change the world takes a group effort. Each one of us can assist in our own way. The stronger the group, the greater difference it can make, and the more difficult it will be for darkness to infiltrate.

We are spiritually of the same eternal quality as God. But, God is Infinite and we are infinitesimal. This means, however, that we are also one with each other in spiritual characteristics. Our bodily externals, such as race, nation, age, and sex, are all different, but these are temporary as our body is also transitory. Other things such as our creed, culture, etc., can change according to our likes and dislikes, which themselves can be fleeting. Or, they change along with the course of an aging body. Yet, our spiritual quality stays the same. That which is temporary is but part of the illusion, and that which is eternal dwells in the spiritual reality. You must become accustomed to perceive and identify with the spiritual reality. All else comes and goes, like the days and nights that pass before us.

The more we understand this, the more we will see that in the spiritual perspective the only lines between us are those that we manufacture in our own minds. No one is born automatically hating those who are different. We are often born in a most fragile condition, but are sustained by the love of our mother and father. We are all born in an accepting and loving mood. We are later trained, from bad association, to despise those who are different. We are also trained to fall into the mindset of sectarianism, racism, sexism, etc., by those who are caught up in the depths of the illusory energy. It is true that we need to learn right from wrong, but this often includes prejudices that are inherited from our fathers, or other members of our society, who have acquired the wrong impressions. This needs to be corrected if we are to employ this 11th commandment, and bring the world into a new paradigm of peace and cooperation. We need to develop a new level of concern for each other. This can be achieved by attaining a new way of perceiving one another, as outlined in this 11th commandment.

There needs to be an emphasis on religious scripture that is truly enlightening. Religious scripture is meant to assist us in awakening our perception of our real spiritual identity. It helps us awaken our natural love for the Supreme Being who is waiting to reveal Himself to us. This inner observation of our real spiritual identity, and of our eternal connection with God, is the *great realization*. Perceiving our spiritual similarities and the underlying unity between one another is the *great recognition*. This means that we recognize each other as we really are; someone that is beyond our temporary bodily externals or distinctions. Given this awareness, our deeper characteristic of divine love itself is the natural motivation for one's participation in spiritual pursuits and to share them with others. This is in direct contrast to the scripture that induces people to follow its rules due to fear, intimidation, or peer pressure that so often deteriorates into fanaticism, fundamentalism and persecution.

When you encourage others to follow this 11th commandment, and as people begin to understand the depths of it, there will be a natural diffusion of peace, cooperation, and mutual respect for one another. In order for the world to be delivered from darkness and imminent war, this code must be implemented. It should not be put into action by force, but instead by the natural growth of society, by higher intellect and reasoning, and by recognizing that this is the higher path for human beings. After all, *your devotion to God is recognized by your respect for God in all beings.*

THE GREAT RECOGNITION

Just as the sun appears as a reflection in countless jewels, so the Lord manifests as the Supersoul in the hearts of all living beings. Just as the sun is located in one position of space, and through its light it can be reflected everywhere; similarly, the Lord is also reflected as the Divinity and the cause of all life in all conscious beings.

With this perception, a person who is spiritually advanced, or one who can use his or her intelligence properly, can recognize that all living beings are parts of the Supreme Being. You can also see that everyone is within the Supreme, and that the Supreme is also within everyone. Thus, a person of wisdom sees all beings equally. This means that beyond the bodily distinctions, everyone is a spiritual being, whether they are a priestly sage, a cow, a dog, a deer, or a lowborn individual. Such differences are of the bodily distinction only. It is a matter of seeing the various living beings within different forms of dress. The dress is the physical body that we temporarily wear for a time. Even within this lifetime the body changes from childhood, to youth, to old age, and then to death. So, even the appearance of this one body is always changing. Thus, it is never something upon which we can or should base our real identity. It is not who or what we are.

For persons who know that all beings are the same on the spiritual platform, feelings such as envy, prejudice, or partisanship do not enter their mind. It is only one's consciousness and mental projections that cause one to focus on our external differences. These bodies may have different shapes or complexions, but within each body are souls that are the same in spiritual qualities. Just as fire is the same in quality, no matter whether it is a single flame or a candle, or a fire so enormous that it encompasses a whole forest, the spark of the soul is the same in whatever kind of body it may exist. Thus, a spiritually advanced person sees the spirit soul everywhere in all species, and recognizes the power of God wherever he or she looks. In this way, such a person is never out of touch with God, and he sees the spiritual energy of God everywhere.

One who has achieved this great recognition sees all manifestations of energy as displays of the power of God. Such a person sees the same quality of all souls in all living beings. Thus he or she can see all living beings without distinction. This is the great recognition.

THE GREAT REALIZATION

We are all manifestations of the Supreme. This Supreme Being is situated in our own bodies as the Supersoul. Understanding and perceiving this is a part of the great realization. Someone who is aware of the *great recognition* understands that spiritually we are all the same, while someone who is aware of the *great realization* perceives God within each and every one of us.

One who has reached this level of realization rises above the typical mental patterns of people in general, which is distinguishing one kind of body that is agreeable, beautiful, rich, and desirable, from another kind of body that is disagreeable, ugly, poor, and undesirable. But, for one who has attained the great realization, such a person rises above material attractions or repulsions and regards everyone as the same. After all, essentially these bodies are just different arrangements and configurations of the same material elements of earth, air, fire, water, ether, etc.

As one continues to advance in this understanding, one can also rise to a higher degree of the great realization. This is the perception that within the heart of every living being is the residence of God. Wherever the Lord is situated, it is a temple. Thus, the wise, seeing the Lord in every being, respects all living entities.

In this way, a person should respect every living entity according to that being's position. In other words, you have to be practical. This means that you may even respect a snake as one of the representations of the Lord's energy, and you may also recognize God in the body of the snake as the Supersoul. A snake is a being that functions in a specific way, helping maintain a balance in nature. That is its purpose. However, recognizing that a snake is also a soul covered by a body, this does not mean that you go and casually pet it. It will still act according to its nature, and will bite you. Similarly, you can respect a lion as a representation of the power of God. In this way, you recognize that the Lord is equally in the heart of the lion, and that without a soul the body of the lion would exhibit no consciousness, however low or undeveloped that consciousness may be. But, this does not mean that you carelessly do something like welcome such an animal into your house. It may be a spirit soul within that body, but it will still act according to the nature of its body and consciousness. The lion does not have the intellectual facility for spiritual understanding as do human beings. It is like a forced servant of nature, meaning that it acts in the way it is supposed to, and assists in maintaining the balance of nature by its instinctual behavior.

In a similar way, we must recognize people who may have criminal tendencies, or who may have a consciousness little better than an animal. That person may also be recognized as a spirit soul enveloped by a material body, but if he is encumbered by an undeveloped consciousness, he must be dealt with appropriately and confined in his actions, or he will harm others as well as himself. What is best for the person's development, as well as the protection of the rest of society, must be considered for his or her advancement. If we use the human form of life solely for the pursuit of animal propensities, such as merely eating, sleeping, mating, and defending, we are wasting the opportunity of human existence and are committing what could be called spiritual suicide.

In the great realization, imbued with a pure heart, you will see the Supreme Soul within all beings. You will also see that the Supreme Soul within you is untainted by anything material and is present everywhere, both within and outside of everything. A person is considered truly wise who can attain this realization and view all beings with the understanding that the Lord is within each one of them. Such a person, endowed with spiritual vision, who can always see the Lord's presence within all persons and creatures, can rise very quickly above all bad tendencies, such as rivalry, envy, abusiveness, etc. Thus, such a person becomes a friend to all, and God is always very near to that person. Such a wise person soon gives up the bodily conception of his real identity, knowing full well that he is first and foremost a spirit soul within the body. This process of spiritual development wherein one attains the great realization by utilizing one's mind, words, and activities for realizing God within all living beings, is said to be the best possible method of spiritual enlightenment.

Furthermore, those who liberally and naturally share this knowledge with others will certainly attain the favor of God, for it will help open the spiritual dimension to all others here on Earth.

In conclusion: a person who sees everything in relation to the Supreme Lord, and who sees all beings as His parts or extensions, and who sees the Lord within everything, never hates anything nor any being. One who thus sees all living beings as inner spiritual sparks, having the same spiritual quality of eternal nature with the Lord, becomes a true knower of things. Thus, how can there be illusion or anxiety for him?

When you realize this 11th commandment so deeply that it becomes as clear to you as seeing the sun rising in the east, then you will know a unity with all life. You will feel a certain oneness with the universe, and with God, and you will know a happiness that has no bounds. Life itself will turn into a new level of reality, and it will become a new step forward in the adventure of existence.

CURING THE GLOBAL CRISIS

As we proceed with understanding the depths of this 11th commandment, we will also begin to recognize its potential in affecting the planet. We can easily see the suffering that goes on in the world, such as the mistreatment or even slaughter of innocent people at the hands of rival tribes. Or, we can see how children are required to serve in military services, and then are compelled to kill other children at the hands of demonic political forces. Or, we can observe how local gangs of youth kill other young people, as well as the elderly, for status or some useless objective. Also, we can witness how people of one religion fight with people of another. These problems, like many others, are escalating and not decreasing. These sorts of difficulties are often a result of emotions that are out of control in people who have a misdirected aim or understanding of life. This 11th commandment is, thus, not meant for one religion. It is a part of the universal spiritual truths that are meant for everyone. Thus, there is no reason why anyone from any religion cannot begin to utilize this commandment. In fact, every religion should add it to their basic list of necessary principles to live by. If all people could begin to understand this unifying perspective that is being shown to us in this commandment, then the necessary changes in the consciousness of people could begin to pave the way towards increasing peace and greater understanding, and, ultimately, promote a greater respect for all beings.

This is the need of the hour. There is no greater need at this time. The planet has the means to produce all that we need in order to live, but anyone can see that humanity does not have the cooperation to share and manage things properly. Yet, with a greater degree of spiritual perception and altruistic thinking, there could be an enhancement in humanity that could change the world, and, thus, make way for harmony and respect for all. If we begin to see our inner similarities, we also begin to see that we are all connected to the Divine. Realizing our intrinsic link to the Supreme and our connection to the rest of the planet and all beings therein, then why should we not be able to exhibit a greater degree of affection and compassion for one and all? We must care for the welfare of others, and then subsequently act with compassion towards the goal of uplifting all living beings.

Everything we do has a motivation that is based on our consciousness. With that motivation, our intelligence becomes involved in making a plan of action, which then is pushed forward by our emotions and desires. Proper motivation depends on proper perspective, which also depends on the correct development of our awareness and consciousness. The higher our consciousness evolves, the higher will be our motivation to act compassionately, and the desire to seek involvement with the causes we feel are worthy will also increase. Our consciousness is developed according to the level of knowledge and wisdom we imbibe, and also according to the practical realizations that we reach because of them. If all that we learn in this life is how to acquire a trade, earn money, participate in politics, and so on, and we do not give enough attention to our spiritual progress, then how can we reach the level of a genuinely developed human being? How can we be more than a society of intellectually enhanced animals fighting over our status, resources, position in the food chain, or over race, religion, and culture? This is not sufficient for us to reach the real goal of human existence.

It is apparent that most people do not know the value of human birth, or do not show it. Thus, they waste their time doing little more than catering to the needs of the temporary body, and to the demands of the mind and senses. In this way, the eternal spiritual needs of the soul are ignored. Thus, they live what appears to be a fully active life, but often without attaining any form of tangible enlightenment or higher awareness. Therefore, many unnecessary problems and complexities of materialistic existence are forced into their lives. We need to implement this 11th commandment in order to start a spiritual revolution that can realize a change and upliftment in the consciousness of all beings.

This is what is needed if we want a happier humanity, and a more peaceful and harmonious world. At some point, people are going to have to demand it. The leaders of this planet who are swayed by different military factions will have to move out of the way to let the common people live in peace. The military is important to protect the freedom of the people, and the country, from invaders, but it should not be the primary interest of the government, or of its budget. It should be a means of maintaining a peaceful society, but not at the expense of the real welfare of society. It does not matter whether these are leaders of nations, leaders of tribes, or leaders of religions. If they are not abiding by the universal spiritual truths, as represented in this 11th commandment, then they will likely be influenced by their own prejudices and favoritisms. This will keep them from having the fullest intention of well being for all humanity in the center of their hearts and actions. Their consciousness will still be too low to exhibit spiritual maturity and fairness for all people everywhere, or from any background. They will still judge people into the groups of those who are "saved" and those who are "lost" or "condemned." They will not see that all people are actually children of God, creations of the Supreme Creator, on different steps of the stairway to reach the Supreme. In such a case, real peace will not be possible.

In this process, religion can play a part in magnifying the good qualities and positive characteristics in people. But, if it is still a religion which honors only certain people, certain paths of devotional expression, or particular ethnic groups, while ostracizing or condemning all others, then it is a religion that still divides people and obstructs a genuine spiritual understanding of our real identity. Every religion should remind its followers of the inner similarities we all share. If this is not done it will still promote divisions based on bodily differences, and, thus, emphasize what are but temporary distinctions. This, in fact, is what a genuine spiritual path is supposed to help us rise above. A religion must be influenced and guided by the deeper science of spirituality. Otherwise, religion can nonetheless remain a means of confinement that keeps people from understanding their real spiritual identity and deeper similarities with all others. It can even prevent people from being sympathetic to those who are outside of their own little group or tribe. This will certainly hinder global cooperation and harmony. This also limits the contributions that could be made to all beings from that religion.

Naturally, everyone may think their religion is the best, and there may be valid reasons for that. This is natural. But, if someone thinks that his religion is better than everyone else's and that other religions are all inferior to his, and that he is so much greater than everyone else because he belongs to a certain denomination, then he has just trapped himself in the world of duality. In other words, as religious as he may think he is, he is not going anywhere, neither to heaven nor to the spiritual domain. Why? Because, being attached to a label, or certain identity related to a group, religion, ethnicity, or any other bodily attachment, is caused by ego, and such false ego will trap a person in continued material existence. Attachment to your temporary bodily identity is based upon false ego, and false ego will stifle your spiritual growth and keep you from reaching a higher consciousness. We must free ourselves from this perception of divisions if we think we are going to reach heaven or beyond. Such divisions do not exist there, but only in this material world of duality. This means that your own mentality will keep you here for however long you continue to maintain such a perspective. These labels of Christian, Jew, Muslim, Hindu, etc., though they may relate to a certain spiritual process, have no bearing on the ultimate spiritual platform, except that they will act as boundaries to your own spiritual development if it separates you from all others.

So, if we are going to reach the height of spirituality, we must be able to rise above this trap, and leave the world of names, labels, and divisions behind. Why? You cannot rise to the spiritual dimension while holding onto the boulders of materialistic consciousness, which cause the perception of superficial differences between all of us.

The only way you are going to get to the spiritual strata is by completely spiritualizing your consciousness. That takes daily practice, just as a daily shower is necessary if you are going to stay clean and free from emanating foul body odors. It takes practice, just as a professional piano player must also practice every day. If he stops for a day, he notices the difference. If he stops for two days, his audience notices. If he stops for three days, then everybody notices. The same goes for one's spiritual practice. We must continually work at recognizing our spiritual identity and the similarities we share with all other beings.

When we actually begin to perceive the reality within this 11th commandment, then we will also understand the responsibility we have to conduct ourselves in a way that will honor it. More than a commandment, it is the next step that society must take in its perception of the universal reality that exists all around us. We must act on the duty of this newly acquired wisdom. If we do not understand this, and cannot change our lives accordingly, then the idea of comprehending higher spiritual knowledge will remain only an idea, never fully manifesting into a reality that we can actualize and perceive in a practical manner.

This 11th commandment also announces a crucial time for humanity's development. If we cannot progress to a stage where people everywhere can understand this commandment, then society could slide into a state of being in which there will be only moralistic principles, the reasoning behind which will be slowly lost. Thus, by propounding these principles to people who don't understand them, they are likely to be hardly followed.

After all, we can see at the conclusion of a fierce battle between different cultures or religions wherein many have died, that the next morning you will hardly be able to tell the difference between those of one side and those of the other. Without uniforms, they are all merely men who had tried to find justification for life, and the means to defend it and survive. Would it not have been easier if they had worked cooperatively with such common goals instead of having fought against each other? This is indeed possible, which is the premise of this 11th commandment. All it takes is a change of perspective, a change of consciousness.

This change must be our goal. The change must come from within our hearts. It is our responsibility to do this for ourselves, for our own progress, and for the whole human community. If the future is bright, positive, and peaceful, the whole world will experience the benefit. If not, then we will all witness a persistent increase in suffering as the consciousness of the general mass of people declines, and as the complexities and problems of life continue to mount.

Every individual needs to participate in creating an optimistic future for the planet by implementing positive spiritual changes within themselves. We cannot simply expect others to do it for us, or wait as if someone else should show the example. The path is being shown to you right now. It is up to you to take it. There is no harm in adding the means to attain a broader perspective of spiritual reality to your life, and there is no harm in forming a closer connection with your fellow beings and with God. At least we can all try to have an effect on the planet in this way, whether we seem successful or not. For, even to move a single grain of sand on the beach is to change the face of the Earth. Sometimes we do not know the effects we have on those around us. So, let us keep those effects positive, compassionate, altruistic, and spiritual. This is the start of the revolution for changing the mass consciousness. That is the key to changing the world.

CHAPTER THREE

Identifying the Higher Self

One of the first steps in further understanding the 11th commandment is to clearly identify the higher self, meaning the soul. We have to differentiate the soul from our ever-changing body. To do this we have to see through the various material elements that comprise our physical form. The body also changes from childhood to youth to old age and then dies. So the body is temporary and not our real identity.

All of us are essentially living entities in different forms. The crucial understanding is that you are not your body. Your true identity and your real potential is always far beyond that. They are outside the limitations of the physical form that you temporarily inhabit. The body is but a useful tool, an amazing machine, but a machine nonetheless.

If we were simply mechanical products, or merely robots, then material development would be all that is necessary for our own contentment. But, we are more than that. Otherwise, why would we feel inspired by viewing a beautiful sunset, or by hearing a great piece of music, or by seeing an exchange of love between others and ourselves? Thus, we need more than external objects and situations to be happy. We can begin by realizing the fact that we need inner fulfillment to be content, which is based on positive emotions, impressions, and actions. This is more than mere bodily sensations.

These bodies that we experience come into existence, remain for some time, and then are annihilated when the body is mingled back again with the earth. Different types of bodies and species of beings are but transformations of the elements that are distinguished by name only. They are like pots, all made of the same substances but named differently according to their various shapes and characteristics. Otherwise, all bodies are created and subsequently grow from the material elements, formed of atomic particles, and returned to the elements when the soul leaves. These bodies become animated only due to the presence of the soul. The bodies may appear to be real, but by witnessing the temporary nature of these forms, we can see they have no permanent existence. Thus, they can be compared to the unreal dreams we have in the night, our involvement in them we take as real, but only as long as we do not awake from them. Rising to the spiritual reality of our real identity is like awakening from the dream of temporary material existence.

The body is like the carrier of the soul, yet the soul is different from the temporary body and is not subject to material conditions. Thus, descriptions such as: stout and strong, black or white, fat or thin, educated or dumb, beautiful or ugly, weak or sickly, are applicable only to the body but not to the soul, which is above all such labels and conditions. Thus, the body is like a vehicle being driven by the living entity within.

To identify the higher self, we also have to see beyond the varying states of our mind and emotions. In trying to understand our real selves, many people are convinced that this evolves around our likes and dislikes. We may spend much time in trying to determine what kind of music we like, or what kind of career we want, what kind of education we should have, what kind of clothes we wish to wear, all of which we hope will make us happier and feel more complete. It is all a matter of accepting a type of identity we wish to portray in this world. However, the mental platform is most flickering and the mind itself is always changing its likes and dislikes. The mind may even change its religious outlook from one path to another, depending on what information we have acquired. Even such feelings as mental or physical distress, thirst, hunger, fear, desires for material happiness, feelings of being old, attachment to material possessions, anger, lamentation, and identification with our body are all transformations within the body and mind. However, these are not applicable for the soul that is free from all bodily and mental conceptions. It can be easy to identify ourselves according to the dictates of the mind, but the real self is higher than the mind. We have to go deeper than that to experience the stability and changeless nature of the eternal soul. Only then can we even get a glimpse of our real identity as the soul.

By experience we can understand the difference between the soul and the body. For example, in a dream a person may witness his own body being killed somehow or other. Thus, we can understand that his actual self is separate from the dream experience. Similarly, while we are awake one can see what is happening to our body; therefore, we can perceive that the soul, the witness, is distinct from the body it observes while being inside of it. Thus, we can begin to understand that the soul is not born with this body, nor does it die with this body. When the pot is broken, the air inside of it returns to the air. Similarly, when the body is broken and dies, the soul becomes free from such confinement.

In this way, because of the body that we wear, which has been created from the temporary material energy, sometimes we think that we are a man, or a woman, or a child, a youth, or a dying person. These all change according to the way we see the bodies we have. However, we are actually pure spiritual beings beyond such temporary labels. Both the soul within the body, and the Supersoul expansion of God which accompanies it, are of the same spiritual quality, although the soul is finite and the Supersoul is infinite. Yet, there is an eternal relationship between God and the soul. Thus, when the soul gives up its attraction for material existence and again turns to the Supersoul for guidance, the soul regains its original spiritual position.

Therefore, through discriminating logic, one should clearly understand the unique position of the soul and thus refute one's misidentification with the body and material energy. One should cease all doubts about the real identity of the soul. Neither the material body, nor the senses, nor one's mind, nor one's intelligence or false ego, all of which can change from moment to moment, can be considered the identity of the eternal soul.

The soul's nature, in essence, is to love and be loved, and to serve its lovable object. This is quite obvious even in our day-to-day experience. The instinct to love is within everyone and, due to that love, we engage in serving and working to satisfy those we love. We become happy by making those we love happy. Therefore, it is recognized that our natural constitutional position is to serve the object of our love, and the ultimate lovable object is the Supreme Lord.

Every living creature is engaged in serving someone else, or they are engaged in serving their own bodies, minds and senses. Thus, the constitutional position of the soul is to serve, but in the material world the entity engages in serving its own purpose for sensual and mental happiness, which involves serving what is illusory and temporary. For this, the living being receives very little benefit or appreciation in return. A person will serve a wife, or a husband, parents, teachers, government, employers, etc., or a person may serve the dictates of his own mental and sensual desires, all with the idea that happiness can be found. Of course, in the material atmosphere, no one wants to be a servant. Everyone wants to become the master or controller of his surroundings. But this is an illusory mentality because even if one thinks he is so powerful, he still remains a servant of the material energy.

For example, when death comes to take you, you cannot escape. You may be so proud and think you are so beautiful, rich, powerful, and independent, but that does not matter. When death approaches you, your position is finished. You will be forced to bow and surrender to the power death has over you.

On the other hand, the Supreme Lord is the source of everything, including the ultimate loving relationship. Since the living being is a spiritual part and parcel of the Supreme, that loving relationship is natural. He always accompanies us as the Supersoul in our hearts, and He looks after us as the Supreme Father. However, He also allows us the freedom to search out material existence for our so-called happiness until we finally understand that the highest form of bliss comes from Him. Then, when we realize this and turn our attention directly toward Him, He paves the way for our continued spiritual progress. In other words, there is never any question whether God loves us or not. His love is constant and more than we can imagine.

Being a spiritual entity also means that we are naturally part of the spiritual atmosphere, where complete knowledge and bliss exist eternally. However, while in this material world, a person easily forgets his spiritual, constitutional position and then tries to be happy independently. In this endeavor, he works to adjust his material situation for personal gain and gratification. This is all due to illusion under the spell of false ego. Ego is there in the sense that "I am," or "I exist." This sense of existence is real. But the false ego is affecting us when we think that "I am this body," or "I exist as this material form." Or "I am white, black, fat, skinny, American, Russian, etc." This is based only on our perception of our material body. In such an unsteady situation within the material energy, the living being experiences such things as attachment and then desire. If desires cannot be fulfilled, such feelings then develop into anger, envy, lamentation, anxiety, or even hatred. A person also undergoes the threefold miseries, which include those brought about by one's own body, by other living beings, and by natural causes. In reality, such feelings are completely absent in the pure spirit soul. So, false ego means the attachment to what is unreal, or what is temporary. If we are truly connected to what is real, or the spiritual strata, then even if we lose everything, our position will remain steady. But, if we have an attachment and desire for what is temporary, and then we lose it, we think that our position is most uncertain and we will feel completely distraught. What is unreal is the temporary, which is everything that comes and goes. A person of wisdom does not become attached to that which is ephemeral.

In order for the living being to remain content within the material conditions of life, he must forget his real identity. Otherwise, it is not possible for one to be satisfied with material activities, and undergo the constant ups and downs of life while ignoring one's natural, spiritually blissful condition. How else could one be satisfied in the pursuit of acquiring such flickering material pleasures? Anyone who depends on the external situations in their lives for happiness will never know true joy, because our surroundings are always changing and, thus, creating insecurity. There is always insecurity and fear when you are not sure of what the future will bring. And in the material world, the future is always unsteady and changeable.

Once you are established in your true nature, you will be able to ascend above all the difficulties in life. This does not mean they will not happen, but they will not influence you in the same way as before, and they will not affect you as they do millions of others. We are suffering because we are not in our natural state; we are like a fish out of water that can never be happy while outside our natural environment. No matter what you do for a fish, only when it is in water can it be content. Similarly, as spiritual beings, only after we regain and realize our spiritual nature will we truly be happy.

If people could actually see their real identity and the happiness within, they would immediately realize their mistake in accepting the material body to be who they really are. They would also realize their eternally blissful relationship with the Supreme Lord. It is for this reason that the living beings should direct their natural loving tendency toward the Supreme Being. Thus, their loving propensity can become spiritualized and fulfilled. Such fulfillment is reached when the living being understands that the Supreme is the topmost lovable object and then begins to endeavor to regain his or her loving relationship with the Supreme. This spiritual loving relationship is ultimately all that can completely satisfy the self. That is the soul's natural state.

While reaching inward in this way to taste the soul's spontaneous happiness and bliss, one should begin to desist from the lusty engagements of the material senses. Just as one who has arisen from a dream gives up the false identity of the dream body, one who is enlightened in the great realization, although living in the material body, sees himself as beyond the body. Unfortunately, a foolish person, while situated in the temporary material vehicle, identifies with such a form and thinks the goal of life is to satisfy the mind and senses, just as one who is still dreaming clings to the dream body.

Therefore, we can understand that all living beings are the Lord's eternal, fragmental parts that are temporarily placed inside various material vehicles to pursue their own level of desires and evolutionary development. The ultimate development comes from realizing your true spiritual identity within.

CHAPTER FOUR

Recognizing the Divine Within You

Regardless of our external condition, we are always connected with God. It does not matter whether we are poor, forlorn, without friends, lost, or if we seemingly have everything we could ever want. These are all surroundings and conditions of the body, and they have little to do with our real spiritual identity. Deep within all of our material surroundings, including our own body, we exist as a spiritual being. We are also part of the Divine, and the Divine as Supersoul is also within us. This never changes. God is always waiting for us to turn towards Him. He gives us the time and the choice of when to do that. When we finally turn towards God, He gives us the inspiration of how to proceed.

All that really matters is how we use what we have for understanding spiritual knowledge. This includes not only using our possessions, but also how we use our time, finances, talents, abilities, as well as our own mind and senses for understanding the Supreme. The more we utilize our life in this way, the more our consciousness becomes surcharged with spiritual energy and the perception of the all-pervading spiritual dimension. As we begin to see how the spiritual world surrounds us, just as the light of the sun brightens everything, or as radio waves that may be imperceptible to our eyes become detectable anywhere with the right receiver, we can also perceive how our essential spiritual identity is an eternal part of that dimension. This is the strata wherein we can perceive our eternal connection with God, and wherein the complexities of material existence seem neither so imposing nor really so difficult. This is the inner life wherein we awaken to the real joy and love we long to experience. Every conscious being is essentially spiritual, beyond the layers of the temporary body, mind, and intellect. All of us belong to that spiritual dimension which is waiting to be revealed, depending on our sincerity.

It is due to our acquiring spiritual knowledge and developing intense love for God that we can progress in such a way to see God within our own heart and in the heart of all beings. It is God's causeless mercy that He accompanies everyone through all stages of life, no matter what is one's material condition. When we can understand and perceive this, we will never think we are alone, or that God does not care about us, no more than we may think that the sun disfavors us only because it has become night. The sun is always there and will reappear just as God is always there and in the heart of all beings. He reciprocates with us to the degree to which we offer our love. The more we call upon God, the more God reveals Himself to us.

That with which you are seeking a relationship and have always sought a deep connection is fully spiritual and within you. It is eternal and not bound by material limitations, either in emotions, reciprocation, or in time. It is that for which you are looking. But it is equally within every other living being as well. Through spiritual knowledge you will be able to see this. You must rise to the level in which such perception is natural and automatic. That is the great realization. Otherwise, while merely focusing on bodily and temporary differences, your consciousness is still far from spiritual.

By recognizing who we really are, as spiritual beings, the false and useless aims of life can be corrected, and then peace in human society will be in order, both individually and socially.

CHAPTER FIVE

Seeing the Divine All Around You

The 11th commandment also means to see the Divine everywhere. When we see the Divine in all living beings, then through that vision we can be peaceful. When there is peace in every home, then there can be peace throughout society, in the whole country, even all over the world. The more you see the Divine all around you, and the more others do the same, the more the spiritual energy and the divine kingdom will manifest on Earth. This is a prime reason for this awareness to be taught at this time.

Ultimately, nothing and no one is separate from God. However, not everyone may reach such a perception in this lifetime. Everyone progresses at his or her own speed. Nonetheless, to the degree that a person sees different values or identities according to variations in the type of body one has, then to that degree a person is still dreaming in the bodily conception, although apparently awake, like one absorbed in a dream at night. Due to incomplete knowledge and a lack of spiritual perception, such a person is still waiting to awaken from the dream of temporary materialistic life. Thus, he remains motivated for various kinds of sense gratification, and remains attached to the illusory glitter of the material world. Absorbed in a variety of materially based value judgments, he clings to his vision of what is good or bad. He is covered by the illusory identification with matter. However, if he associates with those who are spiritually advanced, and opens his consciousness to a genuine spiritual perception of God in all things, he can still change and make progress.

All of creation emits a vibration of energy. Everything has a frequency that can be heard or felt if one's awareness has been elevated enough. This vibration pervades the whole material manifestation and beyond. Yet, it divides into different levels or frequencies according to the elements and species of life through which it emanates. In other words, everything around us, including ourselves, has a particular vibration that exudes from us, and within which we exist. Lower beings and inferior elements have lower tones, while higher beings emit and exist in higher frequencies. These frequencies are essentially various levels of love. The higher the vibration, the higher the love field in which one exists.

In this way, the whole of creation, and all beings within it, are connected through the interaction of these vibrations. The universe is merely a material manifestation, and an extension of the source of the spiritual vibration from which everything emanates. That source, the Supreme Creator, is the key to our being. In other words, everything is but a display of the energy of God. Therefore, God can be seen in every particle of the universe including the physical, the subtle, and the spiritual levels of life. The more we see God everywhere, the more our love also increases for all creation. The more we remember the source of all things, the more our connection and love for the Supreme will also grow.

Through this understanding and perception we can begin to see how the spiritual elevation of one being helps pave the way for the progress and betterment of all other beings. In other words, as one person progresses spiritually, it makes it easier for others to do the same. As one person advances, it has an overall influence, however great or small, on the ability of others to follow the same course, and to benefit from the higher vibration that begins to pervade the universal atmosphere and society in general. In this way, the overall vibration is brought to increasingly higher levels for all beings.

So how can we recognize God all around us? We can especially appreciate His power, beauty, and energy. We can see examples in such things as the sun, moon, fire, sky, wind, water, useful and beautiful animals, worthy and spiritually advanced people, and the Supersoul situated within all beings. Later, a person advancing in spiritual awareness will see everything as a dynamic manifestation of the energies of the Lord, and, thus, a reflection of the Lord Himself in everything. In this way, such a person can see God at every step.

As we become more advanced spiritually, then not only will we become more accustomed to seeing God within ourselves, but we will also become more acquainted with recognizing God all around us. Thus, our spiritual vision broadens, our consciousness expands, and our awareness becomes more refined. We can understand that just by a small portion of God's energy He pervades everything. Plus, everything we see is but a manifestation of His potencies. He is the ultimate source of all. Thus, all that we see, all beautiful and mighty creations are but a display of the Lord's powers.

In time, we can see that God oversees all the worlds of the universe because none can live without His supervision and arrangements. He witnesses all the actions of all living beings in past, present, and future realms. The Lord arranges things in a suitable manner to accommodate the needs, interests, or what is deserved by the living entities within the universe.

In this way, for one who sees everything in relation to the Supreme Being, and sees all entities and energies as His parts and extensions, never hates anything or any being, nor is he or she ever lost from God. In such a perception, that person is always near to God and God is always near to him or her. For such a person, contentment, peace, and happiness are found everywhere, and he can help bring the same insight to others.

CHAPTER SIX

Seeing Our Inner Unity

The 11th commandment also guides us toward seeing the unity that we all share on the spiritual level. Often times we define ourselves through particular traits that separate us instead of unite us. We see each other as having different objectives rather than needing the same resources and necessities for survival on this planet. We see each other as adversaries instead of members of the same team. We see our differences rather than our similarities. The reason for that, for the most part, is that we have yet to discover our true identity, or recognize that part of us which is beyond the ever-changing nature of the material world. We have yet to perceive our spiritual foundation, which is the key to unlocking the mysteries of our true purpose in life. We have not understood how we are all related and connected. This understanding is the key to solving the political, religious, or cultural wars. It is also the means for working together to remedy the economic or even environmental problems that we face. We have the choice to either evolve with purpose and civility, and with conscious intent, or we can choose to remain loose, fragmented, and going in different directions for various reasons. If the latter is the case, this ultimately brings about our own destruction by allowing the seeds of confusion, chaos, and quarrel to grow to the point where they are beyond our control.

However, seeing the inner unity and spiritual connectedness between us and all other beings is part of the great recognition. The first step in understanding this perception is that ultimately all living beings, or all souls, are manifestations of the Supreme Being. All material and spiritual energies have their source in the Supreme Creator. Thus, without the Supreme Creator there is nothing. We are all sons and daughters under the same

God. So, in the light of our spiritual unity, we can perceive that we may be encased in all kinds of various bodies, but the soul is beyond all that. Each soul has the same spiritual qualities. These qualities include such things as being eternal, full of bliss and knowledge, imagining only what ought to be imagined, desiring only what it ought to be desired, and feeling no sadness, anger, or envy. The soul is completely spiritual, it hankers after nothing material, and it is beyond all bodily differences or characteristics.

Furthermore, one who has attained the great recognition does not see living beings only in terms of their bodily differentiations. Instead, he or she sees that inside the body is a spirit soul, a part of the Lord. In this way, a wise person will see the Lord along with his own soul. He will also realize that each individual soul is an expression of the energy of the Supreme. Thus, such a person views all living beings as ultimately united with the Supreme, just as the sun's rays are united with and expanded from the Sun. Through this example, we can understand that the one Supreme Lord is the ultimate cause, and the ultimate shelter, of all living beings throughout the creation.

When we take away the masquerade of that which we think we are, or who we think we should be while in this material body, then we will discover that deep inside we are all the same. As we progress in our spiritual vision, we will recognize that essentially we are all non-different from one another, and that each of us are eternal beings and servants of God. Such distinctions as enemies or friends belong to the external world of bodily activities and mental projections. Recognizing the inner and deeper unity we all share is certainly a reason for peaceful relations, and for cooperating together to make life easier for all of us in a world where many people have to struggle and work hard to survive.

Real unity is found in uniting together in various ways on the path to God. This is real unity in diversity. Why? The reason for this is that we are all servants of God in our spiritual constitutional position. We can either serve Him directly, or through His various energies, such as serving humanity in an altruistic fashion. In this way, engaging in various types of devotion to the Supreme, all of us can feel united. Such activities go far beyond any differences in regards to race, creed, culture, sex, age, nationality, or anything else related to the temporary body. There is only one main goal in human life to be accomplished before we die: Learn how to see God in all things, and subsequently, how to render loving service to God.

For those people who continue to grow and raise their consciousness to higher levels of spiritual perception, the apparent difference between religious and spiritual paths, and their ultimate purpose, becomes increasingly less pronounced and obvious. Those who are spiritually sincere will more easily recognize the primary common goal of each individual. Thus, they can get along with and respect those on other spiritual paths who are similarly just as sincere. They may even assist each other in raising their consciousness and spiritual awareness, though they may be participating in what appears to be different religious functions.

The point to understand is this: There are many levels of energy and vibration. Spiritual energy is the most refined level of energy that exists and resonates at the highest frequency. In the process of material creation, the spiritual energy begins to devolve or condense into increasingly thicker levels of energy and lower vibrations to first produce the subtle realms of existence. This again thickens until it produces matter and the various material substances and elements that make up the material worlds, as well as the forms of the various species of living beings. This in turn has the densest levels of energy and resonates at very low frequencies and holds the least consciousness. This is the present stage in which we exist. Thus, the material energy may condense even more where the hellish, chaotic worlds or states of being are found. Even on this planet Earth, there are various levels of heavenly or even hellish and chaotic realms of existence.

However, now that you are here, the purpose of a genuine spiritual path is to allow you to develop your consciousness so that you can regain your spiritual perception and awareness. At the most complete stage, it is meant that you regain your spiritual qualities and characteristics. This is the ultimate basis of your real identity and constitutional position as a spiritual being. This is accomplished by raising your consciousness to the frequency of the spiritual world. The more spiritual your consciousness is, the more you can perceive that which is spiritual. The spiritual path you take, and its ability to purify or raise your consciousness, will make the difference in your ability to navigate through the material and subtle forces. It will ultimately raise you to the spiritual plane, beyond all material influences, eventually reaching the absolute spiritual domain. This is the essential point and goal of any genuine spiritual path.

So, a true spiritual path or process will give you the complete method to attain your own spiritual perception. A path that only gives hope by its rhetoric, without deep insights or inner changes, or without the purification of your consciousness, is an incomplete path. Or, the path is being given to you by a teacher whose realizations and knowledge are incomplete. It is up to you to make the necessary adjustments, so that you have access to the fullest knowledge available in order for you to reach your most developed potential in spiritual awareness.

While taking the first few steps, faith may be a prime motivator, but faith alone will not be enough to save you or bring you to the stage of enlightenment. It is like climbing a tall ladder; if you cannot take the first few steps yourself, you should not expect to merely stand there while thinking someone else will carry you up. You can start with the faith that you will reach the full height of the ladder, but the steps and activities in your progress must be made by you. You must save yourself. You must be the one to follow the instructions properly, and to endeavor to change your own consciousness, thus attaining the perception of the spiritual connection between yourself and all other beings. You cannot expect anyone else to do it for you. Furthermore, you cannot use someone else as an excuse for your own deficiencies or why you did not do better.

A further consideration in seeing our inner unity is that if everyone is a part of God and God cares for all living beings, we should not think that God does not accept the devotion from someone following another spiritual path, even if the spiritual process seems different than ours. Do not think that God has not given His word to other nations or other people, as found in additional sacred texts. There are many portions of the great universal spiritual truths to understand. Similarities exist between one spiritual path and another that may come from different parts of the world. It is but a declaration of the glorious nature of the one Supreme Lord, and the fact that we all equally share a spiritual identity as parts of God. This is another part of the great recognition, that we are all sons and daughters of the same Supreme Father, Creator, and Benefactor who supplies His children with what they need. It is the responsibility of each pious individual to attain this great recognition of the inner spiritual unity that exists between all of us. If each one of us is a spiritual manifestation of God, then God has a purpose for each of us. He views all of us as His parts and parcels, or sons and daughters. He is merely waiting for us to realize this. A merciful God would never manifest beings only to later cast them away forever. To think such a thing is merely the way humans project their own weaknesses and ignorance on God. In reality, we cannot fathom the depths of the Lord's kindness, mercy, patience, and love. They are all beyond our means of comprehension.

This spiritual knowledge that is now being given to you is provided so that you can more easily find your way back to God and recognize God all around you in your daily life. Not everyone is lost in the same jungle, or exists within the same consciousness. There is no single path suitable for all. Everyone has to find themselves, and realize their own spiritual identity in their own way. Thus, there are particular paths most suitable to accommodate the differences in people, depending on their position, past, level of consciousness, abilities, and intentions.

On the absolute transcendental plane of existence, divisions of the spiritual domain and different types of devotional service to God are not recognized as points of contention. What is recognized is the variety of ways to perceive and relate with God. There may be differences in prayers, names of God (all of which refer to the same Supreme Being), sacred clothes that are worn, articles used in worship, designs of houses of worship, etc., but the object is the same--to express our veneration and gratitude to God and try to please Him. All the different forms and facilities for various types of worship can bring a joy and happiness that unites one and all in the process of glorifying God together. This is the spiritual domain that could manifest here in this world, if it were not for the blindness of humanity. This blindness separates humanity from the light of the spiritual strata, and it keeps them bound in the darkness of materialism through unnecessary friction and divisions. It is up to mankind to end this quarrelsome, war-like consciousness.

Therefore, it is not good to force a particular outlook, or a single religion, on everyone when such an intention only further divides and agitates society. This does not produce the principle of respect for all, and it counters any progress meant for attaining the great recognition. But, one must be naturally attracted to a process, and naturally grow with a path that will take one to his or her next step in spiritual development. Otherwise, the spiritual progress that one seemingly makes, if based only on the judgments and dictates of another whose consciousness has not been highly raised, or on the approval of a dogmatic institution, is but shallow and pretentious. Instead, they should be the genuine realizations that are truly needed to make a difference in our personal lives. The great realization of the presence of God within each of us and the great recognition of our inner unity between one another is not to be artificially declared by some cleric or oneself, but it must be an inner actuality and perception. For example, when a person feels the difference in relief from hunger after eating a nice meal, the realization of that satisfaction, and the means to attain it, is no longer a subject for debate. Similarly, spiritual realization must also be as clear as perceiving the relief from hunger. The freedom from sensual desires is the first sign of one's genuine spiritual advancement.

The worldly aspect of religion, meaning the rules, regulations, and observances, are insufficient if they do not lead one to the door of spiritual realization within. If a person is outwardly religious and moral but inwardly still spiritually inexperienced or ignorant, or if he remains absorbed in materialistic desires and judgments, then he is just like a child that is trying to act like an adult. Worse still, if one pretends to be spiritually realized or even says he has contact with God, and, thus, requires or demands respect for himself, yet remains spiritually undeveloped, he will only mislead others and can even stifle their growth. Such a person becomes a disturbance to society and often, due to his own selfish interest, works to enhance his own profits or adoration, or instills hatred toward other religions, rather than endeavor to genuinely fulfill the spiritual needs of others. Such a person may preach for more donations, more converts, more power, but may say little about genuine spiritual knowledge and awareness due to his own lack of experiencing such things. He will often demand that everyone follow his path while shunning and criticizing all others. Thus, the potential in the world for peace, understanding, and respect for all becomes minimized. Furthermore, struggle, quarrel, and even war, can result from these attitudes because more people will follow the same line of thinking and adopt the same level of immature consciousness. Thus, genuine social progress becomes stifled, and we lose the means of seeing our interconnectedness on the spiritual level. Then we are left to wallow in our own increasing darkness. Humanity has suffered in such a way long enough, but must choose to leave this sort of rut behind. Thus, the 11th commandment expects you to raise your consciousness and perception above such shallowness, and to move forward--closer to spiritual reality. Within the awareness of such spiritual understanding we can see our inner unity with all beings. This vision is what brings a true and positive change to the whole planet.

CHAPTER SEVEN

Opening Our Hearts to One Another

When we begin to see our inner similarities, meaning the spiritual connections between us, we can start to be more considerate, respectful, understanding, and open with one another. After all, we are all reflections of God. We are all rays of light whose energy comes from the same powerhouse, like sparks that are all lit by the same fire. We are all looking for a niche, a place where we can fit in and are accepted, welcomed, and loved. We all share the same concerns and needs for food, shelter, and clothing. We all look for peace and security in a world that often seems to offer little of either. We all have our stories to tell of our experiences in this world, and each one of us offers areas of learning or expertise that can help others make this world a better place. For this reason, we should be able to respect and open our hearts to each other.

Fear often keeps us from being open or respectful towards one another. There are different types of fear. There is the fear that someone will reject us and make us feel as though we are outsiders, or that we are not good enough the way we are, and that we need to change. There is the fear that we may open ourselves up too much to other people, and, thus, become vulnerable to those who might see our weaknesses, and then show their criticism towards us. Or, additionally we may fear that we may like someone, only to learn that they may not like us in return.

Furthermore, because of past mistakes we may be stricken with a sense of shame or worthlessness. This may incite us to rectify our faults, which is positive, but if it is directed in a negative way in which we may become bitter and angry, it becomes a barrier between God and ourselves. For example, for some reason we may feel dejected. We may feel that God dislikes us, or that we are unworthy of God's attention, or anyone else's for that matter. This may broaden to the point that we feel we have nothing to offer that God or anyone else would appreciate. But, such self-pity is a product of our own false ego, and it is part of the illusion from which we must break free.

Part of this illusion includes the way in which we view other people. This may involve developing many wrong impressions from which we form improper opinions about someone. It could even cause us to build up anger and dislike toward a person who may not even feel the same way towards us. Even if they are averse to us, we should be willing to open ourselves to appreciate whatever positive traits they may have. We should not be willing to carry anger in our hearts. A grudge can get very heavy after a while. It becomes a burden that we do not need, like extra luggage that we have to drag along with us wherever we go. To rid ourselves of such anger toward another being, we should concentrate on the good qualities and characteristics of that person. Everyone has some good in them. Everything has a positive aspect to it. So, even challenging people and difficult situations can teach us the means to practice patience and tolerance.

An orange fruit gives orange juice when it is squeezed, because it only has orange juice in it. Nothing else is expected from it. But, what happens when you are squeezed, or when you are tested by someone or by some challenging situation? If all you have is love inside of your mind and consciousness, then when you are squeezed or challenged, all that will come out is love and compassion. But, if anything else comes out of us, such as anger or bitterness, then it is a lesson for us to know where we need to work on ourselves. Thus, situations that arise, or people who may squeeze us in such a way, all act as our teachers. We merely have to look for the lesson contained within each encounter. If we do not view it like this, we may allow our anger to rise up and hateful words may pour out of us, which will create negative impressions in others as well as ourselves. Then, we may feel ashamed, and rightly so. Impressions that we create about ourselves to others are very difficult to change, and correcting them may take many good actions in order to counter the negativity we have inflicted on others. This is a way of learning about our weaknesses that need attention.

There is nothing wrong in recognizing and honestly admitting our weaknesses, and then putting a genuine effort into correcting them. It is far more harmful to pretend, or to try to forget our defects, and go on denying them and acting like we have no faults. We all have weaknesses of various kinds, and we have to forgive ourselves for them, just as we have to forgive others. We also want God to forgive us for our mistakes. Therefore, we should try viewing others as we would want God to view us. We have to learn from our lessons, from our past, and with greater determination move forward and work to free ourselves of such faults and weaknesses.

As we look at ourselves in this way, we must come to realize that, in essence, we are all reflections of each other. We are all very similar. You are a reflection of me, and I of you. Thus, there is no reason to be afraid of talking to each other because there is always something that we have in common. In fact, there are many things that we have that are alike.

The further manifestation of what can be called the great recognition is that each soul in all beings is the same in quality. This is also a universal awareness, a higher spiritual perception of an international brotherhood and sisterhood of humanity. This is long overdue. It is the preliminary step in bringing about a global effect of God consciousness. It is a means of practical cooperation in assisting one and all in material necessities and resources, as well as in spiritual well-being. This is a part of the great recognition between us that the 11th commandment recommends.

The whole purpose of any religion remains unfulfilled if this 11th commandment cannot be realized and utilized in a practical way in our relationships with one another. It is a manifestation of our regard for all of creation. Otherwise, the whole process of religion is but a romantic and sentimental attachment to the idea of being rescued or redeemed in the name of a savior or scripture. In actuality it results in something far less. If the spiritual dimension cannot be manifest in one's consciousness in the here and now, do not think that person will experience it after death. The entertainment of the idea that we will attain heaven or the Promised Land merely by faith, regardless of how divisive and spiritually immature we are now, is misleading and an illusion.

Likewise, when there is war and terrorism over religion, and fanatics kill bystanders to promote their own creed or agenda, it is like offering God the mangled bodies of His own sons and daughters who may worship Him in a different way, or who may not be inclined toward worship at all. This does not mean that He wants to see them suffer, or wants them to become victims of those who are unreasonable and immature in their own spiritual understanding. This will not win the favor of God, regardless of what your religious leaders may say. If they say that acting cruelly toward others who may be on a different path is what God wants, they are in fact misleading you into the darkness of spiritual ignorance, which includes the lack of understanding the real reactions of your own activities. Such overzealous people are no better than those who may not worship at all. The spiritually immature may kill while thinking they are doing God a favor by ridding the world of such people and, thus, earn a place in heaven. But how can they think this way? Why would God want such people in heaven with so much blood on their hands, and so much cruelty in their hearts? How could they find a place in heaven when they cannot begin to make heaven on Earth? They fight and kill for their own religion and do not see that God accepts all forms of respect and worship that is genuine, heartfelt, and done in sincere goodness. Even if worship of God is done differently than the path you have taken, He still accepts the sincere mood of the worshipper. Such genuine devotion will bring benefit to all others, and not leave them with despair. Honest worship of God in any manner is that which leaves the onlookers or participants with inspiration and encouragement, leading them toward the great realization, which is to perceive God in all beings. So-called worship that leads to the anguish of others is hell bound.

God wants everyone to worship Him, not for His benefit but for one's own blessings. He accepts worship of all kinds that is respectful of others, purifying for the society and our consciousness, and is cooperative and caring for all beings. But, worship and religion that expands by the blood and death of others only increases the pain and suffering of humanity. This is only a man-made religion and is painful for God to witness. It is like blood offerings to God that make the lap of Mother Earth a place of suffering. It does not help to establish heaven on Earth. It does not help to spread God's true interests in the world for the benefit of humanity. Thus, it is unwanted, and in time it will be forced to perish.

Let us throw out those religious belief systems that are the cause of a divisive mentality, which create the seeds of war. Let us follow the universal spiritual truths that free us from war and hatred. This 11th commandment is the basis of that spiritual truth. If we really look into our own spiritual essence and disregard the conditioning set in our minds, if we search for our selves before our regressive or faulty mental impressions were fed to us through the media, or before bad association or faulty or fanatical religions colored us, we can see that we all have an inherent innocence. Just as a child is innocent when it is first born, so our spiritual essence remains unspoiled by any material conditioning. In reaching a spiritually mature position, we rekindle that innocence. In other words, in that spiritually elevated consciousness, we can look at things differently, purely, without all the clutter in our minds clouding our view of those around us. In that state of awareness, we can also see the way in which our own mind can project its problems, prejudices, bitterness, or shame into our view of others. When such qualities affect us, this is when we make those around us the cause of our problems, or how we blame negative situations for being the reason for the way we are, if it is not to our satisfaction.

We often fail to accept the fact that, regardless of how things have gone in our life, we can change our situation, or ourselves, especially by learning from the difficulties that we have experienced. From such things we can learn what not to do to others, or how to overcome our difficulties. Then such tribulations may actually be great blessings for our development. For, is it not the case that a person will never truly appreciate a good meal until he has known hunger? Or that a person will not really appreciate money until he has known poverty? After that even the little things in life may be viewed as great blessings, and we will more easily accept the difficulties that helped develop our character into the way we needed to be, especially if it was necessary to do something important. Such significance does not have to be great, and it may have a positive impact that may go unnoticed even by us. Yet, it may also change someone, and, thus, the world, for the better. That may be all we are meant to do in this lifetime. Or it may indeed be the case that we do something that has a much greater impact on the world.

In this light, the 11th commandment also inspires us to see and feel the pain and suffering of others, and to assist in doing something about it. There are enough resources in this world to provide for the necessities of those in need, if they are spread around and not dominated by the elite or greedy. Especially in regard to natural catastrophes, we must recognize that we need to work together and rise above cultural, racial, or national differences if we are going to rebuild the community and lives of people. When seeing others in dire circumstances we must know that "there but for the grace of God go I." The same things could happen to us, so we must help each other. We should feel that "good enough for me" is not good enough. What is good must be good for everyone. We must help others attain their needs as well, in whatever way we have the capacity to do. We are all children of God, children of the Earth, and in that respect we are one people. You cannot bring the spiritual vibration and energy into this world until this is realized. And that starts with each and every one of us.

When there is a higher regard for others, and more love and compassion shared by all, then people, families, and communities are all happier. They are more successful and have the means to reach higher potentials. When there is a lack of such regard for those around us, when we criticize and demean those with whom we associate, then people are not happy and often not as successful. They are more likely to have a limited view of themselves and not see the higher potentials they could be capable of achieving. By exhibiting our darker character in the form of anger, envy, hatred, or insulting and spiteful words, we cut ourselves off from our real nature and from our real identity, and from our higher potential. When we see others in this condition, we should have compassion for them, just as others should have compassion for us when we are in such anger or unhappiness. We must understand that we, in essence, love all beings. Anger and hatred may give us some impetus to act, but in the end it is not satisfying. Anger and hatred are like a bowl that has a small hole in the bottom of it. It may look quite promising and pleasing at first when it is full, but in the end all it offers is emptiness.

Compassion is the quality of genuine concern for others. This is exhibited in our motivation to wish all beings the highest welfare, and then act in a way to manifest that concern and that positive attitude. Then that person can share in the uplifting expression that benefits all of us.

We must try to see the good in everyone, not just the faults in them. Positivism will spread uplifting thoughts and outlooks. We can dislike the imperfections but not the person, in the same way that parents may love their son but not the drunkenness if that is his habit. So he may be loved as a son, but his position and freedom may have to be limited until he conquers his bad habit. But that is to keep him from harming himself and others. This is done out of love for him, as well as for those he might injure.

You have to see that beyond the skin, beyond its color, inside the eyes, and within the being of every person are their emotional and spiritual needs. These needs, in their essential forms, are simply to love and be loved. Everyone has this tendency to love someone. It is a reflection of the nature of our soul. The soul naturally loves. And that loving potential reaches its highest caliber when it is directed toward God, and to all of His parts and parcels, meaning the spiritual identity of all beings.

No one is born hateful. No one is born without love in his or her heart. No one is born without the emotional needs to express their loving tendencies, which are but illuminations of the soul. It is only when these needs are not met that various means of emotional defenses are developed in order to avoid disappointments, or cover emotional scars, or fend off further heartache and pain. This often causes someone to shut down the person inside that he or she would like to be. It is the main cause for developing various external addictions.

In this way, we are all much the same. We just need to learn to reach in and touch a person inside, and recognize the emotional needs of that person. This is the way we also fulfill our own requirements for expression. We must help others in order to help ourselves. Loving and caring for others allows us to rise above our own problems, which certainly makes whatever difficulties we appear to have seem much less significant. There are few rewards greater than tending to the cares and needs of others, knowing that they are also children of God, and that if we can lead them closer to God, then the Supreme will also look more kindly toward us.

We must recognize that life in this world is often not easy, and most people are doing the best that they can with what they have. We may not be able to fix everything, or mend the hearts of everyone, but we can recognize what we can change and plan how to do that. The more we can work to fulfill the spiritual needs of others, the more complete they will become, and the more the spiritual dimension will manifest in this world. The more we depend on God, the more we can allow God to work through us. If we sincerely act in this way, we can, indeed, expect miracles.

CHAPTER EIGHT

Utilizing Higher Consciousness in Everyday Life

As you progress in developing your spiritual consciousness, you should become more aware of the difference it makes in your everyday life, and how you apply your spiritual perception more frequently in all kinds of situations. It must become a means of making practical improvement in the way you conduct yourself. It also becomes a means of how you view a broader and deeper perspective of your purpose in life, your purpose in the world, and your affect upon the lives of others.

For starters, you must begin to see all things, whether stationary or moving, as forms of energy manifest from the Supreme. Your family, friends, nation, the planet, and everything are combinations of elements and energies that are formed by the power of the Supreme Being. Therefore, everything you see, including your own self, has its connection with the Lord, and exists within that connection; just as a strand of pearls depends on the string that holds them together.

Nonetheless, the material energy is always changing, and on the physical level we must also participate in that principle of change. In this way, your material identities, namely the body in which you live and relate through, and the bodies of all others, are always in a process of flux in various ways. Through such methods as direct perception, logical deduction, studying descriptions in spiritual texts, and especially by your own realizations, you should clearly understand that this material creation and everything in it is temporary. It has a beginning and end. It is not the ultimate reality. Therefore, one should live by carrying out one's duties on this material platform, while at the same time not becoming unnecessarily attached to them, knowing there is still a higher or more refined realm of existence in the spiritual domain that we need to reach. Thus, with such a perspective, one moves about in this world freely, friendly to all, engaged in all kinds of activities, yet cheerful and content in spiritual consciousness. Even while engaged in maintaining one's own body or house and family, by understanding the temporary nature of material things, a person of wisdom remains free from falling into the illusory aspect of it all. By disconnecting from the bodily and material concept of life, one can delve deeper into experiencing the happiness of the soul. The spiritual dimension is where we can find the stability of real contentment, joy, and happiness that is not susceptible to change at any time. This lies outside the effects of the constant dictates of the mind and demands of the senses, which are often motivated by the ungrateful masters which are never satisfied, namely lust, greed, anger, and envy. The mind and senses are the domain where these masters exist, and they motivate us to act on the material and sensual platform, within the temporary bodily conception of life.

By maintaining our spiritual perception and consciousness, and always recognizing the supreme truth around us, you can be free of the illusory influence of the temporary material conception of existence. One who is wise should therefore endeavor to decrease what can become the overwhelming waves of complexities of material existence, and keep one's life simple to enjoy the natural bliss of the supreme truth within.

In utilizing a higher consciousness in daily life and in dealing with others, there are a few additional basic principles we need to incorporate into our character. These will be quite natural for anyone who is absorbed in the spiritual perspective, but until you have attained that status, you may have to keep these in mind. These include:

1. Be merciful. A person of wisdom is merciful to others by understanding their plight, perceiving their lack of spiritual understanding, if such is the case, and trying to provide the means so they can acquire it. This also means to be kind to all creatures, knowing they are also parts of God. In this way, such a person does not cause unnecessary injury to others in mind, body, or

spirit. Thus, he or she does not engage in insulting or injurious talks that may create pain. Such a person always acts in the best interest of all beings.

2. A person of wisdom is also tolerant and forgiving. He or she knows that everything is temporary. Just like the way something agreeable is followed by what is disagreeable, in the same way the winter and summer seasons follow each other. So, a wise person does not get caught up in unnecessary expectations, although he remains steady in his responsibilities. He is also quick to forgive others, knowing that insults or injuries that may be directed towards him are received only by the body and mind, but he, as a spirit soul, is separate and, therefore, above such things. So, he does not have to accept such actions from others in a personal way. In this world it is natural that there will be misunderstandings, try as we might to make ourselves clearly understood. Even if someone is belligerent or offensive, a person of wisdom treats everyone fairly, and knows that it is better to see one's own self truly than to care so much about how others see you.

3. A person of wisdom always remembers his own spiritual position and identity as a spirit soul within the bodily machine. He knows that the nature of the soul is to be an eternal servant of God. Thus, he or she maintains the universal spiritual truths as the foundation for his or her standards and values in life.

4. By being fixed in this truth, such a person also remains free from envy, or being unnecessarily desirous of any person, possessions, or position. He remains steady and balanced in material happiness or distress, fame, or infamy. Nor does he become overly excited or depressed by the ever-changing material events that go on around him. Thus, he remains undisturbed by the material desires that push so much on the average person, and in this way he stays free from many of the selfish or sinful activities that capture the attention of so many, along with the resulting complexities that follow.

5. Furthermore, seeing the temporary nature of the material world and all that is within it, a person of wisdom remains free from possessiveness for unnecessary things outside the basic

requirements of life. Thus, he stays free from the constant endeavors to acquire money to buy newer prizes or to maintain a higher status of material happiness and prestige. He only accepts what is needed to keep himself healthy and fit, and can, thus, remain free from trivial and unwanted entanglements. Therefore, a person of wisdom enjoys a higher degree of peace and contentment, not suffering the disturbances that affect those who are absorbed in material pursuits for pleasure under the constant dictates of the mind and senses.

6. Fixed in spiritual consciousness, a person of wisdom is patient and fearless, knowing that regardless of whatever difficulties may arise, ultimately truth prevails and the Lord's plan will manifest. Thus, he remains thoughtful and free from doubts, focused on the goal of life.

7. In business, a person of wisdom does not try to cheat others in order to acquire temporary wealth or power. Nor does he encourage others to become absorbed in bodily pleasures and motivations that bind one to the illusion of flickering material existence. Thus, he also remains free from gambling or questionable business ventures. These kinds of activities can take one down the dark alley of anxiety, anguish, and unnecessary intrigue and scheming, which can certainly lead to dishonesty in business relations and other areas of one's life. On such a course, no one will be peaceful, trustworthy, or have a balanced mentality.

8. A wise sage is also unhappy to see the unhappiness of others. He knows that all suffering comes from contact and identification with the illusion, whereas real freedom and happiness are attained in the reality, or that connected with the spiritual dimension. Thus, he tries to give the chance for everyone to reach the spiritual truths wherein freedom from miseries and distress can be attained.

9. Finally, one additional quality a person of wisdom has which helps him or her to remain poised, balanced, and focused is to accept and recognize all of one's assets, benefits, comforts, or good fortune as the blessings from God. Whatever we have, great or small, that is of beauty, wealth, power, or even the simple facilities that help make life easy, often comes to us outside of our

own influence or because of the assistance of others. Or, it may come from our own intelligence, but only from the good graces of proper teachers, and with the blessings from God that we have a good brain. Thus, we must be thankful. If for some reason we may have many benefits that others do not, we avoid becoming proud of them, knowing full well that anything material may leave us as fast as it once appeared before us. We come into this life with nothing, and we certainly take nothing with us when we die. This thought alone should make it clear that everything we have in between these two events of birth and death are but temporary conditions.

We are but travelers in a world that is in constant change. Being aware of the temporary nature of everything certainly helps one remember his or her real spiritual position. We are reminded that everything is but a display of the energy of the Lord, to whom we should be thankful, because He provides us with what we have that assists us through life. Thus, rising above the temporary and into the eternal spiritual dimension should be the obvious goal of life.

CHAPTER NINE

Identifying Our False Self

One of the core points of the 11th commandment is that we perceive our higher selves, or our spiritual identity as the soul. However, seeing the reality of our higher self also means to distinguish it from our false self. We must learn to recognize the false self and its motivations. The false self is the ego-based image we have of who we are. It is the impression we have of ourselves in connection with the body. It is defined by the way we look, our physical size and shape, our skin color, our material status of life, and the drama that goes on around us. It is also the image of what and who we would like to be, and how we want to appear in the material world. It is that image which allows for little, if any, security and stability, because it is based on the impermanent and ever-changing nature of the world. In other words, in this temporary material creation, things can change at any time, such as what we are, how people view us, and what we have, especially at the time of death. It can be worrisome that after we succumb to death most people do not know where we go afterwards. This is our position if we accept the idea that our material body is our real identity. But we must realize that this is a false conception of who we are.

This temporary material body is like a foreign dress that we are born into. Thus, we get used to it and think that this is the basis of our whole identity. However, it is but a vehicle that facilitates our material desires. It is a machine that gives us the means to chase after our longings, depending on the level of consciousness that we have developed. Thus, every type of entity in any particular species is provided a body that is suitable for assisting it in that particular being's function and level of consciousness.

When overcome by the urge to act according to one's material bodily identity, one forgets his constitutional position as a spiritual being. He then makes plans to enjoy the world through his mind and senses in whatever ways seem agreeable to him. Thus, one becomes ignorant of the real self within the body and works, sweats, laments, sheds tears, or enjoys due to the conditions that the material body experiences as they are interpreted by the mind.

In this way, we can see that in the human species of life people get involved in playing roles like actors on a stage. They often become very much attached to the activities of the characters they assume. One person may be a mother or father, or a daughter or son, or have a career as a doctor or lawyer, or he may consider himself to be a Russian or an American, black or white, and so on. These are the types of roles people may play in life, based on such things as the type of body they have, or mental makeup, character, desires, or the place where they are born. Some people play these roles so well that they become very much attached to them as the basis of their identity and purpose in life. Thus, if they are parents and their children grow up, or if they have a career and their job ends, then they are no longer what they have always considered themselves to be. Life then can get confusing and difficult. They may go through an identity crisis as they are forced to change the view they have of themselves. However, one's real spiritual identity is beyond all such false conceptions.

It is like the dreamer who is absorbed in whatever scenario takes place in his dream. He may even think that he is a completely different person. In this way, someone can become completely lost in the labyrinth of bodily identification and materialistic existence. While absorbed in this mental projection, a host of good or bad feelings may overwhelm him based on his accomplishments or failures, including joy, happiness, exhilaration, pride, or anger, envy, disappointment, and even hatred. This is all due to the numerous situations in the drama in which a person may identify. Those who are filled with such emotions and engage in actions or outbursts based on these feelings are themselves oppressed, afflicted, and even controlled by these kinds of thoughts. It is as if they are kept prisoners by their own low consciousness, being destined to the deprivation of genuine happiness and the freedom from the actions and reactions that materialistic endeavors create. They are stuck with this mindset unless they can break free and enter a higher degree of consciousness and spiritual awareness. We pray that such a breakthrough may happen for all.

Hatred, jealousy, and pride are negative emotions that are the destroyers of our future and our happiness, and which pave the way for further divisions and suspicions between us. The only way to defend us from these destroyers of unity and happiness is through the use of proper spiritual development. Even if we make only a little advancement, if we increasingly become better human beings, more warmhearted, compassionate, and caring for all, this will automatically bring more happiness and meaning into our lives, and to our community and the greater human family. However, we should not expect to work this out over a short period of time, but we should count our work over the course of many years, because that is what it may take. We must not be impatient. We must be determined and sincere to work on ourselves as a journey, an adventure that may take time. Why not? There is nothing greater that we are meant to accomplish. Everything else is ephemeral. Our own spiritual development contributes to the greater good of the whole family of this creation. The more who participate in this process, the more the spiritual dimension will be invoked into this earthly existence.

If a person is angry, then he or she is suffering, and those with whom he comes in contact, such as wife and children, will also suffer. Whenever such a person is overly angry or unhappy, he may become a dangerous person for himself and those around him. If he is not happy, he certainly cannot make others happy, but will likely cause others to be miserable. The more he understands this, the more he will want to be calm, compassionate, and warmhearted so he can be happier and kinder to those around him. When we can see the difference that our attitude and disposition makes, the more we will be convinced that anger and hatred are not only bad for our health, but also leads to unhappiness for ourselves and those near us. It also leads to a dark future. It is a product of misidentification. Thus, a person should transform the mind by right thoughts with a foundation of spiritual awareness and insight. By implementing this in our daily life, year after year, the transformation will take place in increasingly deeper degrees for real benefit and development in realizing one's real spiritual identity.

Unfortunately, it is the nature of common men who are spiritually unaware to try to be satisfied in the illusion of temporary material existence. Thus, in order to be happy, they acquire various possessions that are essentially here today yet may be gone tomorrow, like a newly built beautiful house that can unexpectedly get turned to ashes by a fire. These sorts of goals set themselves up for the roller coaster of ups and downs that are guaranteed within the drama of the bodily concept of life. Compared to the eternity of the soul, one lifetime is like a lightning flash. However, using one lifetime in spiritual pursuits can bring one a giant leap forward toward entering the eternity of the soul, and freedom from such highs and lows that come from identifying with the false self. This is one purpose behind the 11th commandment.

The first step in recognizing our false self is in perceiving the illusory concept of "I" and "mine." In our natural, spiritual state when we say "I" we would mean "I" as the soul within the body. But, because of our ego, we say "I" to mean our body, and, therefore, think, "I am the body." This is centered around the mind and senses. This is the false sense of self. Then we say "mine" to indicate anything connected or related to the body, or anything toward which our mind feels a strong attachment.

It is like driving a vehicle and getting into a collision with another driver. We may be unhurt but we will still get out of the car and accuse the other driver by saying "You hit me." He might not have hit us directly, but we identify with our car so much that when the car is damaged it is as if we were hit ourselves. It is the same way as our identification with the body we are in. Thus, the concept of "I" and "mine" in relation to the body alone is a product of ignorance.

When you can distinguish your true identity from all of your external projections, attachments, and appearances, then you can begin to become centered in the real you, or your essential, spiritual being, the core of who you are. Then what happens around you is only the drama, like watching a movie. That movie is happening to all the things you may identity with, such as: 1) your wife or husband, or 2) your children, or 3) your parents, 4) your friends, 5) your job, 6) your religion, 7) your house or home, 8) any other attachments you have, or 9) even your own body. Nonetheless, these do not belong to the real you, but are merely items that you consider a part of you. You see these things as a part of your life, and a part of whether you are happy or not. However, when you can distinguish your real self from all of these items, then you can begin to determine who you really are. Then you also have the means to start achieving your own independent happiness which is based on the soul, your real identity, and not merely on the ever-changing material body and its situation.

For example, as previously mentioned, something may happen to your car but not to you. It only happens to you if you identify yourself with the car. This is similar to identifying your higher self with your body or those things around you. Circumstances are happening to your body all the time, but the soul within remains the same, independent and aloof from all the materialistic activities that go on. So once you lose all false identity, then you are free from all mistaken disasters and problems that are based on that identity. You are essentially only spiritual, which can be seen after everything else is distinguished for what it is.

As the body is temporary, then all its relations and positions are just as impermanent. They have a beginning and end. To lose what one clings to always results in unhappiness and misery. Thus, the bodily conception of life is the basic principle of suffering while in this material creation. The person of wisdom will, therefore, understand that the body is never as important as the soul. He or she will put emphasis on understanding and perceiving oneself as the soul in the body. The body is indeed a great and amazing machine and tool that we have, but this machine is only activated as long as the soul remains in the body. Once the soul leaves, the body is no longer needed and becomes useless if not even repulsive as it deteriorates back into the basic elements from which it is composed. Once the body is born, it is already being vanquished within a matter of time. However, the soul will go on.

For this reason, one who has spiritual understanding accepts his body as a proper tool to use while moving forward in his spiritual progress. He knows that he is not the body, but is the soul inside and, thus, accepts the body as a machine that will one day no longer be needed once he can leave it and enter the eternity of the spiritual domain. For a person of wisdom, regardless of what kind of body he has, he does not merely view himself as black or white, or belonging to only a particular race, country, culture, sex, etc. He sees that spiritually he is beyond all that, though temporarily caged in the physical contraption. Nonetheless, the human body is a blessing because it provides the perfect facility with proper intelligence, discrimination, and opportunity for realizing one's spiritual nature. Thus, the importance of human life should not be wasted or taken lightly.

In the conception that the body is our identity, we may cling to those who appear similar to us or who have some relation with us. For example, we may make friends with those of the same race, or same age, a similar culture and country, all due to identifying with bodily similarities. However, at the same time we may dislike all those who are of a different race, culture, country, etc. This counters any means of establishing peace, harmony, and cooperation between any such divisions based on these kinds of superficial differences. Thus, we should see that all these categories based on bodily distinctions are but superficial and not related to the soul. As long as society remains in this type of spiritual ignorance, men will continue to make such bodily differences, which are reflections of their lack of higher awareness that would be expected of a truly advanced civilization.

Modern technology is material advancement, which many people enjoy and for which they pride themselves for the facilities it can provide. However, without accompanying technology with spiritual advancement and inner awareness, society is only becoming half developed, and is missing the true goal of human life. Thus, technological development without spiritual knowledge only helps society more efficiently make arrangements for eating, sleeping, sex life, and engaging in defense and economic development. Is this not but a higher standard of animal life? Of course, ordinary men greatly appreciate developing the animal propensities and seek ever-increasing levels of happiness and pleasure through such acts. However, it is time that society reaches a higher stage of civility.

By perceiving our higher self, and recognizing its difference from the false ego and identification with our body, we should understand that if we do not use the opportunity of human existence for spiritual progress, this life remains incomplete. If we ignore the need for acquiring spiritual knowledge altogether, then this body is practically useless since in such a situation we will have accomplished little more than what is achieved by ordinary animals, though with a little more sophistication. So we now need to focus on achieving something higher.

Furthermore, by understanding the difference between our higher self and the lower self of mind, body, and senses, we can also separate ourselves, to varying degrees, from the stress that may go on around us. There is always some stress in material life, but how we perceive it will make the difference in how we handle it. Even difficult things can become easy by remembering our spiritual and divine nature, and by being conscious that we are parts of the Supreme. We must remember that our real identity reaches its full potential on the spiritual platform. This is the goal. Even difficult situations become easy if we somehow remember our divine spiritual nature and our connection with the Supreme. We can easily remove the emphasis on the temporary role we play in our material existence and align our focus on our real identity. Yet, even the easy things that we do may gradually become a burden. The comfortable situations we have may become stale or dry in due course of time, when we forget our spiritual position and depend solely on bodily stimulations for happiness. In other words, there is only so much satisfaction that such activities can give us before we become tired of them and we feel it is time to give them up for something else in our search for genuine fulfillment.

Even when it comes to giving up addictions and bad habits, when you realize your higher self, the lower self of body, mind, and senses can no longer be so influential in their demands for sense pleasure. By controlling the lower self by the higher self, one is no longer dragged away so easily by the mind's ideas for pleasure. In fact, in time such attractions become tasteless and disgusting after experiencing the higher taste of the soul in spiritual reciprocation with God. Sense pleasure cannot compare, and thus one loses interest in such activities. By gaining control over the mind and senses in this way, one can easily become free from such feelings as hankering, greed, jealousy, or anger. A person of wisdom will certainly see that catering to the pangs of the senses are but artificial needs of the body. They do not interact with nor satisfy the needs of the soul. However, keeping the body fed, clothed, and healthy are not artificial needs. Nonetheless, no matter what one does for happiness, until the needs of the soul are met, one eventually must deal with the feelings of emptiness and unfulfillment, and the longing for newer and stronger thrills for the mind and senses. This can ultimately lead to habits of self-destruction if it is not restrained by attaining a higher spiritual taste.

The need the soul has for complete freedom, beyond the limitations of the body, is to unlimitedly express its spiritual love in fully developed spiritual relationships with God and other souls. As we get deeper glimpses of such relations, it can give us a happiness that knows no bounds, and we get increasingly eager to experience more and more of this reciprocation and bliss with God. In this way, a person of wisdom can easily surpass all the material cravings of the mind and senses, and all so-called pleasures attainable by the physical body within this material creation.

CHAPTER TEN

Our Purpose in Life: Finding Contentment and Joy

Naturally, if everyone had a choice of what they would like, most people would simply ask for contentment, joy, and happiness in life, and whatever items they think would bring that. Everyone is looking for this in various ways. Yet many people get so caught in the complexities of material existence that they often forget this simple goal. Many think that getting more and more money will give them all the happiness they want. Indeed, there may be a need for financial stability, but the endeavor for excess amounts of money often diverts one into more trouble than expected. It also often causes one to miss the real goal of life.

However, if we are really going to try to find peace and happiness we must ask ourselves a few carefully considered questions. First, in order to determine the direction we need to take to find genuine happiness, we must ask if you are the body, the mind, or the soul. Then also ask where you have come from and where you are going after this short life is finished, and why are you here in this material world. Understanding your actual position, who you really are, and what you are actually connected to, is the way to find genuine peace and happiness. Otherwise, the misconception of your real identity is what causes the misdirected aims of society. Subsequently, there is an escalation of competition for the types of temporary happiness based on pleasing the mind and senses that so many others also want. The increase of materialistic activities performed merely to satisfy one's mind and senses does not truly provide a permanent sense of well-being and fulfillment. They often involve actions that may create a short-lived feeling of excitement, but actually cause a decrease in one's sense of real purpose. They may even decrease one's duration of life if such acts deplete one's physical well-being. These materialistic activities may be like nectar in the beginning, but because they do not offer real happiness and lack substance, they become like poison in the end.

People who are attached to such activities in the pursuit of bodily pleasure often have little interest in developing a more sophisticated and refined consciousness for understanding their spiritual identity. Because their mind and senses are uncontrolled, such people are pulled by them this way and that to the depths of materialistic existence. If, however, a person begins to tire of the constant endeavor to please his mind and serve his senses, and he begins to ask why he acts in this way while no longer feeling any real happiness, he will have a chance to climb out of his stagnant mindset and open up to higher levels of perception as a spiritual being inside an impermanent material body.

The only way a person can feel the happiness that one has been hankering for all of his life is by fulfilling the needs of the soul. If the needs of the soul are not met, then the mind and senses will never be calm or stable. They will always go through stages of agitation and restlessness.

The needs of the soul are met by attaining complete freedom from the physical condition and entering into spiritual loving relationships with the Complete, meaning the Supreme Being. As one progresses in this way and enters into a stage of loving reciprocation with the Supreme, he will feel that his life is complete. He becomes satisfied with the blessings of the Lord and feels the highest peace of mind. Being spiritual sons and daughters of the Supreme Father, we will naturally feel blessed and at peace by following His will. He is naturally inclined toward giving us blessings when He sees some sincerity in our devotional mood. On this path, for every step we take toward God, He will take a hundred steps toward us.

This reciprocation and perception, of course, may take some time to develop, depending on how dark or selfish our consciousness has become from years of materialistic endeavors. We can hardly taste the sweetness of fresh fruit nectar if our mouth is filled with dirt. As we clean our mouth, gradually our ability to taste the sweetness returns. Similarly, if our consciousness is always occupied with the pursuit of dark, dirty, and misguided materialistic activities, it may take some time to cleanse our mind of such desires so that we can begin to taste the sweetness of spiritual relations and activities.

If you want to cleanse the mind, you must first cleanse your activities. By taking instruction from those who know, you first learn to hear about God and your own spiritual identity as the soul. Then spiritualize your activities, which cleanses the mind. This also purifies your desires, which is the symptom of the consciousness becoming spiritualized. Then, the more spiritual you become, the more you will perceive that which is spiritual. You will increasingly recognize the spiritual dimension all around you. Then, you will be able to begin to enter into transcendental relations and experience a higher level of happiness and joy. In this way, real happiness is achieved in the eternity of spiritual existence. Situated in divine consciousness, one becomes increasingly distant from the miseries of material life. Such miseries are based on the illusory and bodily concept life. Remember, all suffering exists only within the illusion. The freer you are from the illusion, the freer you will be from misery. As we progress in this way, the sensual desires that once seemed so important and that we have learned to relish so much will become insignificant and even disgusting.

In such consciousness, one's intelligence and spiritual perception becomes steady and one knows peace. Otherwise, there is no happiness without peace, both socially and individually. Real peace is established through one's connection with God, the real friend of all living beings.

Ultimately, you must seek out that knowledge which gives you the most understanding of God, along with His activities, characteristics, and loving personality. Only that awareness will help you rise to the heights of complete happiness and fulfillment. You must search this out from those who know, at least while the world still has those few souls wandering on the surface of the planet who are aware of this knowledge. Only while situated in that awareness can you reach real contentment in your pursuit for true happiness.

CHAPTER ELEVEN

Politics and Leadership According to the 11th Commandment

In applying the 11th commandment to our lives, the way we view politics and the system of leadership we choose will also be affected. When people who are not spiritually inclined, such as those who are atheistic, enter politics and become leaders by hook or crook, the whole atmosphere becomes increasingly covered with nescience and confusion. Such politicians may pose as having affiliations with some religion, but this is often done with a motive of getting in favor with people for the purpose of acquiring votes. Their real agenda is often hidden away and revealed much later. With such politicians in charge, beneficial programs meant for helping the poor, or assisting with educational systems or the environment, often become reduced, cut back or under-funded. Such funds that could be used for the benefit of the taxpayers are then diverted toward military development with the promise that it will make everyone more secure. The nation does indeed need security, but not knowing the duty of a good leader, such politicians engage in threatening and fighting with one another at the expense of the common people's well-being. Then in their distress, society may take spiritual life more seriously as they search for ways to find peace and solutions to their problems and help from God.

These unqualified politicians often mislead people by saying they are providing a brighter and more secure future through military engagement. But the damage done through such violence and destruction often leads to increased expenditures and years of difficulties that are spent recovering from wars and rebuilding what was damaged or destroyed. If society elects such political or religious leaders, they will not experience the relief and bright future they wish for. Such a leader is building a stone boat that is bound to sink along with everyone that follows him. Thus, he and his supporters create a dark future for everyone. In this way, they create hell on Earth and are bound for hell after death. When determining your choices, you must consider your own future, not merely in this present life, but in the hereafter as well.

We can see in this world that there are those who lead people down the road to trouble. They present their untried and unbalanced theories as if they are providing definite answers to problems, but their inner rebellious nature, revolutionary ideas, or plain stupidity, often merely increase the difficulties we already have. Such disruptive thoughts arise in the minds of those who are already so discontent, envious, or foolish. How can happiness arise from discontentment? They plant their ideas in the minds of others who are also restless and dissatisfied, and then try to gain influence. We have seen this happen in the world of politicians as well as in various religious organizations many times, and, thus, misguided people become all the more ill-advised. It leads us farther away from a peaceful and divine life. It prevents us from reaching the real goal of human existence. We often become ever more trapped in a world of divisions. Then our consciousness focuses on our differences rather than on spiritual unity, and, thus, the world weakens into a planet of increasing chaos.

Many civilizations on the planet that have prided themselves for being advanced are not genuine civilizations. This means that they are not as civilized as they think. A true civilized society will hold love, compassion, cooperation, wisdom, and freedom as its basis and foundation, and not mere technological, economic, or military superiority to dominate others. This sort of emphasis in advancement does not solve all the problems of life. It does not promote true peace in the world, nor does it make a society truly civilized. It mostly perpetuates the differences between the members of society, as well as the selfish idea that the privileged can control all situations by the notion that might is right, and, thus, continue to dominate the weak.

Society must pick a true leader, and not merely elect the lesser of the evils among the candidates running for office. But, they must know what is a real leader. A real leader must also know the universal spiritual truths. Then such a leader can make programs that use a foundation that is universally applicable to everyone. In this way, the leader must use a complete philosophy for his politics. Otherwise, an imperfect leader will not be able to create an ideology that is acceptable to everyone, but he will continue to speculate on what might work and suggest ideas that are untried, untrue, and that continue to create confusion. This goes on while he hides the real agenda, which is often to trick people into working hard to pay large amounts in taxes that are funneled away from truly benefiting the people and the planet. If the leader is a fool, the government becomes a fool's paradise.

A real leader must be ethically fit and strong in order to subdue disturbances properly. Before a leader can affect the world, he must take care of things locally, in his own domain. He must first curb whatever sufferings his own subjects and citizens endure. They are supporting him, it is their taxes he is overseeing, and they should be the first to reap the rewards of proper leadership and government funding. So first, all thieves, rapists, kidnapers, murderers, and dacoits of all kinds must be stopped and apprehended. This will help create peace for all honest citizens. Also, programs that benefit the people, such as securing employment opportunities, protecting natural resources and the environment, providing proper health care, etc., must be established or people will lose hope for the future.

Dishonest miscreants and criminals in society flourish because of cowardly and impotent heads of state. If such leaders cannot manage their position properly, criminals make use of the situation to terrorize honest citizens. But, when heads of state are strong enough to curb all sorts of criminals in any part of the country, then they will not be able to flourish. When miscreants are punished in an exemplary and immediate manner, then good fortune follows. Crime goes down, the expense for law enforcement decreases, and then the citizens in general do not need to live in fear. This will positively affect their confidence in government and the way they contribute to the country. However, when laws are passed that protect criminals and force honest citizens to become incapable of defending themselves, or where law enforcement is slow and ineffective, then thieves and rogues become prominent in society due to an incapable government. Such a country soon becomes a dangerous place in which to live. Misfortune is then bound to follow.

Thus, a leader's priority is first to his or her land and citizens. Only after his own area is secure, and beneficial programs are firmly established, should there be any engagement for large expenditures or military action outside of defending his own jurisdiction, beyond his borders, and only then if such military ventures do not unnecessarily tax the economy. Once local problems are solved and adjusted, the leaders and people will have a stronger base from which to tackle challenges and difficulties in other parts of the world.

If a ruler or government is effective in curbing crime in its own country, keeping the citizens free from disturbances of cheating businessmen, corrupt politicians, terrorists, thieves, etc., then by virtue of such a strong leader, he can invoke the confidence of the people and more easily collect taxes. More citizens will be honest and willing to pay. However, if a leader or government cannot protect the citizens from such dacoits in public or government affairs, such an ineffective leader should not be so ostentatious as to think he deserves the right to continue to collect heavy taxes from his subjects. If the leader is ineffective and allows criminals to occupy his jurisdiction, then he will share in the reactions of the evil deeds that are conducted under his regime, and his own future will become very dark. Thus, a bad ruler perpetuates the spoiling of the whole country.

What is worse is when rogues themselves are elected to office. Then such cheaters, taking advantage of their situation and position, will enjoy life by living off the high taxes that are taken from the citizens. Or, they will engage in political or financial intrigue that will put large profits into their pockets at the taxpayers' expense. This in turn makes the people more dishonest by trying to hide their income from being taxed by crooked politicians. Then, as this criminal mentality spreads, trickling down from the leaders, the whole country becomes increasingly corrupt.

The hierarchies and regimes that operate according to self-serving methods that are in fact vicious and unjust, especially toward honest people, cannot remain in place. The ultimate force of truth in the world will see them fall sooner or later. We must bring forth the power of transformation, not by force or manipulation, but by genuine concern and spiritual love.

However, it is not enough that leaders try to provide peace through military domination or force. There needs to be funds that will support educational projects that will spread genuine spiritual knowledge that can invoke a real change of consciousness in humanity at large. This does not mean simply to spread a particular religion, but to spread that spiritual information that can be applied by anyone, anywhere, regardless of religious affiliations. By providing the means for a genuine change of consciousness, and an uplifting growth in perceptivity of our spiritual unity, there can be peace by the deliberate choice of society as opposed to mere military might. There can be harmony through intellectual and spiritual growth. Otherwise, real peace will not be possible. It will only be a strained peace since the underlying cause for disunity and trouble remains, waiting for the opportunity for conflict to break out again.

Naturally, there may be times when military force is needed to put an end to unnecessary conflict or to subdue criminals, but it can never be a means to lasting peace.

Our disrespect toward one another is nothing but a reflection of our disrespect toward God, or at the very least our disconnection from God. Whereas the more our relation with God is established in a mature manner, the more we can see God in everything and everyone. In such a state of mind, war, being a vehicle in which we try to kill as many of the enemy as possible, is like blaspheme in itself. As we continue to lose our connection with God, we lose our moral values, our civility, our care and concern for each other, and then the basis for quarrel and war escalates.

The point to understand is that the elite or criminally minded who live at the expense of others will never bring forth or promote the will of God, especially if it means a change in their own status quo, position, wealth, influence, etc. They will never reflect the unconditional love of God on others but will relentlessly devise the means for manipulation and exploitation of the weak. However, we can change whatever elitist structure there may be, not by ordinary revolution or militant activism, but by merely choosing to not participate in it and by selecting the path of light and love. This is an alternative based on spiritual realization and recognition of the Divine in all beings. The polarization between good and evil will bring forth the distinctions of harmony and balance for those who choose such a path, and darkness and torment for those who choose selfish methods. The path of truth and love has always prevailed in spite of the trials that may have to be endured to reach the goal.

A ruler should be the representative of perfect morality. He should exhibit exemplary behavior in his actions, directions, and speech. Thus, as it is most beneficial for society in general to work toward spiritual advancement, so it is also beneficial for a ruler to work in ways that enhance his or her own spiritual development. He or she should see to it that everyone has an equal opportunity to do the same. This is proper leadership.

Furthermore, proper leaders should arrange things in such a way so there is cooperation between God, nature, and humanity. If we act in a way that pleases God, then He will oversee us and supply what we need. But, that also means we should respect and honor the blessings the Supreme has given us and continues to give us, and exhibit thankfulness by honoring and cooperating with nature. Thus, we will not spoil or overuse our natural resources, and there will be harmony between humanity and all aspects of nature. If our land is full with natural assets, the nation and world can be economically prosperous and comfortable. If we do not honor our resources, or if we spoil them through pollution, or overuse them through bad management, there will be scarcity and high prices. This gives way to apprehension, fear, and difficulties for people who must conduct their lives at increasing expense. Thus, the economic status of the country and the confidence of the people will begin to plummet. This is why there must be proper cooperation between God, mankind, and nature, which is another aspect of understanding the 11th commandment.

If people cannot progress spiritually and see things according to this 11th commandment, they will not make any advancement toward the higher goal of human life. This is beyond ordinary moralistic principles and is the foundation of real spiritual perception and realization. It is a duty of the government that the facilities are provided so this can go on nicely. Thus, if any fanatics from any religion become terrorists toward another, and make things difficult for all, the ruler should apprehend such fanatics immediately and make arrangement for such people to have minimum access to their jurisdiction. Such a consideration may be unfortunate, but it is nonetheless necessary to establish and maintain peace for the honest citizens and those who sincerely try to advance spiritually.

CHAPTER TWELVE

Economics According to the 11th Commandment

People may ask what the 11th commandment has to do with economics. But if we are to see the Divine in all of life, we must understand that there is a way of conducting business between each other that upholds and advances our perception of this principle. Conducting business or managing economics in a way that deliberately cheats or exploits others will harden our hearts and our sensitivity so that we become unable to perceive the Divine in all living beings and even in ourselves. How can we not be careful of what we do when we know that the Lord in our hearts is watching all of our activities?

The point is there must be integrity in all transactions and business relations. If we use the 11th commandment, then by seeing the Divine in all living beings we must realize we are not merely doing business with another person, but we are also conducting transactions with the Divine. This means that the Supreme is also observing our every act, not only from within us but from within the person with whom we are dealing. If the relationship has integrity, then that is fine. We will continue in our spiritual development even while doing our business. But if there is dishonesty and cheating in our involvement, then the quick profits we make will only pave our way downward. This will not be helpful. So we must conduct ourselves, even in business, with the foundation of the 11th commandment in mind.

We have easily seen that companies with power may produce various foods, drugs, beverages, or devices that are said to be of great benefit or are healthy for us, or help us solve our problems with no side effects or unexpected problems. Yet, time and time again we learn that different kinds of products have indeed been pushed on the public and have caused harmful side effects, much to the dismay, suffering, and frustration of the people. However, the company or even the government may deny any such possibility of injury. You must always bear in mind that a story presented as factual from an entity or company whose purpose is power, control, or profits is often a story not to be trusted.

For example, in today's world, to put it very simply, the use of paper currency, which only represents a value rather than being a tangible item like gold or silver coins, may be convenient to the user. But those in positions to set the value on such currency can also more easily manipulate it. This creates abstractions in the link between the paper representation and the actual gold it is supposed to be representing. At other times the combined confidence that people and governments place in a currency may fluctuate greatly, making it especially vulnerable to times of political upheaval or war. Such currency can then become completely worthless, as history has shown.

The fluctuating character of this type of currency also helps separate society from nature. Nature requires balance in the environment to operate properly, while currency that only represents what is supposed to be tangible is more easily manipulated. It is the adjustments in currency and interest values which often create stressful fluctuations for the ordinary consumers and for the general mass of people. People who are most implicated in these fluctuations are less likely to advance economically as those who are in positions to claim profits from the same adjustments or manipulations that take place in the markets and economy. This is the difference between those involved in the global monopoly game, which is artificially propped up, and those that depend on real value, such as the gold standard or genuine real estate values.

In this way, currency that is not based on a real gold-standard is false if it does not accurately represent the reserved gold. Because the money value is inflated, prices on commodities rise. The only way to reduce inflation and have an honest currency is to use that which has intrinsic value, such as when trading something of equal value as in bartering or using real currency like gold and silver coins. That is an honest system.

Real prosperity flourishes on the natural gifts of nature, or God's gifts to us. Villages and towns and their local economy will flourish when there is plenty of grains, vegetables, herbs, trees full of fruits, rivers flowing with fresh and clean water, and hills full of minerals. When this is the situation, there will be plenty for everyone. If society has sufficient natural resources in this way, then why should it endeavor for huge industrial complexes that require the labor of numerous men by sending them into dark factories where they spend their lives in exchange for inflated dollars, and then have to pay a sizable portion of their earnings back to the government in taxes?

Industry produces so many items that are in demand only because of the advertising they show to convince people that they need to purchase the item to increase their happiness. Essentially, the more society depends on artificial necessities, the more vulnerable it becomes to artificial crises. Thus, civilization suffers and the economy slows whenever there is not enough oil, gas, electricity, or when the prices of such modern commodities become too high. When there is a loss of oil, gas, and other such necessities, or when there is an electrical blackout, so many activities are forced to stop. Numerous machines and appliances are but recent inventions, but now we have become so dependent on them that without them we think we can no longer function. Thus, people become trapped ever more deeply in the struggle to earn more money just to buy more things that they are convinced they need in order to live happily and comfortably. In this way, they are tied and enslaved to a system whose goal is profits rather than really benefiting society. In such a system, humanity loses its sensitivity for their finer intellectual development, and has no time and no taste for any spiritual pursuits, except possibly for the most elementary levels of moral standards.

In the natural form of economy, the basic principle of economic development is land and its produce. Whoever controls land controls food. Whosoever controls food and fuel controls the world. This is why land should always be in the hands of local farmers, so everything is shared in a local economy and all people can prosper. Once large industrial or national complexes take it, such large tracts of land are no longer in the hands of a regional economy, but are controlled by large, global enterprises that have their own concerns and plans. Then land becomes another element used to manipulate profits, resources, people, and even other communities and global markets. History has also shown that such companies often acquire more influence because of their connection with crooked politicians or their networks that want more and more power. Thus, they push whatever plans they have for their own interest with little concern for the people of the region. This is the path to darkness wherein the suffering of the world increases in the guise of material advancement.

Quite simply, by developing the land properly for vegetable and grain production, society can solve its eating problems. By producing enough cotton, wood, minerals, and additional resources from the land, humanity can work out its economic difficulties without depending on an artificial economic or political system.

Those who do become wealthy by honest means can more easily acknowledge his or her opulence as gifts from God. Thus, one's business, if done morally, can be a way of invoking the principle of the 11th commandment. Such gifts or blessings also come in the form of one's own intelligence and ingenuity for devising wholesome ideas and needed products for the benefit of others, and from which one's business will expand. Thus, without the blessings of God in every way, we cannot progress or be happy. All things, from wealth, health, good birth, beauty, good education, etc., are all examples of gifts from God. Therefore, we all must acknowledge our gratefulness, especially those who have become more successful. When a family or society offers such acknowledgment, their success and happiness can increase in a decent and moral way.

In conclusion to this line of thinking, we must recognize that one of the greatest forms of pollution in this world is that of competition for position, power, and money. It is natural to work at devising better ways of doing business and producing more effective products. Whoever has what is best will more likely succeed. Competition based on envy, jealousy, and deviousness, or simply for more money, makes individuals and companies resort to dishonorable means to get ahead, to get more market share, more customers, and ways of making products more cheaply. This also adds to social stress by forcing people to increasingly think in terms of growing profits and income. This takes away from the peace in the world, and often adds to the pollution in the environment by using resources in less eco-friendly ways.

Because we have forgotten our true spiritual nature, we are stressed and crying over small and unimportant problems that have little to do with our real identity as spiritual beings. Because such difficulties are not connected to who we really are, they actually have little relevancy to our spiritual nature. But because we are so attached to our temporary and bodily identity, we are affected so much by these ephemeral and superficial troubles. This is not how we are meant to proceed through life. We should not get entangled in this illusion in such a way. It wastes our time and distracts us from the things that matter most.

We may have made so much technological progress and have numerous facilities added to our comforts of life, yet we can still see so many people suffering in this world. This is primarily because money, and people who are greedy for money, rule the world. Not everyone is cruel, but who cannot see how the misery of many people on this planet is caused by the greediness of others? The perverted politicians and rulers in various countries have created so much trouble that most all of the torment of people who are poor, starving, or even being slaughtered or enslaved into prostitution to do the wicked bidding of others, has been due to the unending selfishness and greed for money and power. Do you think this is the way of a truly progressive world? Is this the way of a genuinely advanced civilization? We can plainly see that it is increasingly becoming more godless and, thus, more hellish. If this trend continues, society will lose its moral values and respect for life. People will become progressively more desperate, and the world ever more lost.

A new influence must rise to purify this world from the rulership of money and dirty politics. We must feel the influence of spiritual knowledge, for only then can society know what is real peace and happiness, and live together cooperatively. It is the knowledge and awareness of our spiritual identity and our connection with the Supreme Spirit that will fill our hearts with the deep inner peace and contentment that we are looking for. If we can progress in this way, our own happiness and peace can spread to others. That is how we can become the peacemakers and help fill society with the tranquility of such self-sufficient happiness and contentment. Then our only concern will be how to relieve the suffering of others. The more people who reach this state of consciousness, the more society will become cooperative, harmonious, mutually respectful of others, and beautiful. Then the tendency for war will cease and the world can live in peace. We have to be strong enough to make such a change.

CHAPTER THIRTEEN

Nonviolence According to the 11th Commandment

When understanding the 11th commandment and the need for us to raise our consciousness to perceive the Divine in all beings, it should also be clear that we need to observe respect, kindness, non-injury, and nonviolence toward all. Nonviolence and the path to truth and God are inseparable. Nonviolence means non-hate. We must never hate anyone. Hatred itself is a great enemy or deterrent on the path of the 11th commandment and spiritual progress in general.

In our personal dealings with others there should be no violence whatsoever that would cause physical or mental pain. This means that even our talk should be pleasing, respectful, and never insulting or belittling toward others. Nonviolence means that one should not do anything that will put others into misery, confusion, or distress. Nor should we leave someone in such conditions when something can be done to alleviate one's suffering. If we can provide assistance but do not, then that is a form of violence. Without having compassion for others and without having an understanding of their feelings, you retard your own development and stifle your own journey to heaven.

That which furthers the future happiness of people is nonviolence, which also means that which jeopardizes the well-being of people now and into the future is violence. Violence also means to stop or interrupt one's progress in spiritual life.

In our respect toward other people and other cultures and forms of worshiping the one Supreme Being, violence should never be used in the attempt to establish the superiority of one religion over another, or to forcibly make converts. We must be aware of the value of each spiritual path and what they have to offer before dismissing them. Each genuine spiritual process has the potential to raise the consciousness of its participants to various levels, if they use it properly. A dislike of other spiritual traditions often comes from a mere lack of understanding. Good religions strengthen the positive human qualities and minimize the less desirable ones. They must focus on the good qualities while helping to overcome the bad. If it cannot at least do that, then it is hardly to be regarded as a beneficial religion.

If a religion cannot show its attractiveness by the force of its spiritual purity, but must resort to trickery, bribery, torture, terrorism, or violence and war to make converts or conquer over other religions, then it is not a true representative of God. Nor will it spread the genuine love that God has toward all of us. The participants of such a process never really know God through such methods. If they cannot recognize the Lord in all beings and work cooperatively in such a way, then they certainly will not know the many aspects of God, nor will they be allowed into heaven after death. Death alone does not change a violent and divisive person or enlighten their consciousness to the degree in which they can be qualified to enter heaven. Death alone is not enough atonement. They will still be forced to adjust their consciousness by some other means before they will be allowed entrance into heaven or the higher realms, not to mention attaining the perception of the spiritual domain, which is still farther beyond the realm of the heavenly world. Thus, a violent religion, or a path in which its participants are cruel or hateful toward others, is not a representative of God's hope for humanity. It is not a means to perceive the spiritual similarities between us all that exist deep within whatever bodily differences we may have.

Religion can never be used as the basis or justification for violence against others. Otherwise, it makes that religion an abomination before the eyes of an ever-loving God. How can it be otherwise? To spend our time criticizing or demeaning other religions is to criticize another way of worshiping and petitioning the same God, though the Lord may be called by a different name. Do you think you can enter heaven by showing hatred toward those who love God but show it in a different way, or through a different process? To base one's opinion of another because of a difference in culture or religion is an indication of possessing a lower consciousness. Generally, you cannot rise to heaven while holding the boulders of a low consciousness.

Saintly people will see the divinity in a person and their desire to reach God as best as they know how. If they are sincere, they are worth holding dear as God also holds them dear. God will hear the prayers of all who offer them to Him with love. You must make sure that same love is also in your heart, otherwise how can God hear you if you hold hatred or contempt toward others? Such feelings will misdirect the prayers you submit to God. How can you see God in others if your vision is clouded by differences, criticism, or hatred? No true religion will ever propagate such an attitude or vision. If it does, then how can it benefit its followers or the world? It will only be a cause of quarrel and disunity. This creates a separation from God, not a unity or link with God. So how would God appreciate such a thing? One should run away from such a philosophy and find one that honors the Divinity within everyone, as God is to be recognized within all.

Without genuine love of God, a person cannot appreciate another's devotion, or another's path of religion. He or she will only focus on the differences and solicit criticism. This hinders their spiritual development and attainment of a deeper connection with God. A lover of God can see that God is present everywhere and is reached by genuine devotion to Him in whatever uplifting way it is expressed. This is the stage we need to reach in this present age of higher development so that we can all live in peace and assist one another in reaching higher states of being. This is the way to open the spiritual dimension in the world and in society.

However, in order to maintain a nonviolent and peaceful society, there may be times when violence is justified and necessary. The 11th commandment does not permit murder, slaughter, or war. However, at the same time, justified violence and war are inevitable factors in society for keeping law and order. So to maintain a nonviolent society, violence may be necessary in the protection of oneself and for the good of the general mass of people who wish to live in peace. There may also be a need for warranted violence to maintain moral standards, and to defend such principles against those who wish to bring them down or establish their own violent agenda for power and control at the expense of peace in the world.

To use violence or a weapon in defending ourselves from a criminal who means to do us grave bodily harm is justified. A criminal who has no respect for the life of others will continue to be a disturbance to society. He will go on harming people to gain his own selfish goals. Therefore, he must be apprehended to confine him from acting out his criminal tendencies and violence on others. If he is in the process of torturing or killing someone, or if that is his intent, then there may be the need to exhibit lethal force toward such a person to prevent him from committing further harm.

No matter how much we can recognize the soul within every living being, there will be some who are evil. Not those who are merely mislead or mistaken and who can be rehabilitated, but who have every intent to harm others in society and who are beyond correcting. These include rapists, murderers, child molesters, kidnapers, etc. Their consciousness can be as low as animals in not being able to control themselves or discriminate between right and wrong. These people must be dealt with in an immediate manner and with severity for the protection of the rest of society. The appropriate punishment must be given to curb evil-minded people. How can you expect society to peacefully progress otherwise?

Similarly, there may be nations whose rulers are focused on the design to press forward with their non-spiritual agenda to dominate others, regardless of how people are harmed. Those who are unable to follow the spiritual truths to benefit all must be restrained by force if necessary. At that time justified violence and authority may have to be used to overcome political and heartless cruelty, especially that which is done due to the wicked desires for worldly gain or power for the few at the expense of the many.

This sort of violent but defensive action should be done sparingly, but with the intention that it will correct the situation and help establish an era of true peace and respect for all. It should not be exhibited merely for economic or political gain, or for conquering others. But on the other hand, we must know when to take a strong stand to defend what is morally and spiritually correct, and to preserve those standards. This need of defense against those who are wicked and immoral, as well as impious principles, has gone on in the world for thousands of years and will continue for many more. However, other than in such extreme situations, nonviolence should be our normal temperament, both socially and individually.

CHAPTER FOURTEEN

Diet According to the 11ᵗʰ Commandment

In following the 11ᵗʰ commandment, it expects genuine inner growth, not merely superficial piety. There are expected realizations meant to take place within you, and such a change of perception will lead toward alterations of conduct. Serious adjustments are not unlikely in your own spiritual development.

One such adjustment in further understanding the 11ᵗʰ commandment, and in the need to respect all beings as aspects of the Supreme, includes the choice we make for the types of food we eat. In developing our higher spiritual perception and refining our consciousness, fresh natural foods are the most suitable. They hold the proper nutrients, or as much as can be available in this age, for good health and finer brain development. They also contain fewer toxins and provide a higher vibration that we imbibe for our body and consciousness. Thus, in our respect for the spirit in all creatures as part of the Supreme Spirit, we choose to not eat animals.

There is no reason for killing and eating animals if there are plenty of fruits, vegetables, and grains available. The idea that one cannot live without consuming flesh is only misguided selfishness. This is especially important to understand for one who is trying to progress spiritually. Managing land properly in order to abundantly produce grains, vegetables, fruits, etc., will solve the hunger problems of humanity. This will be enough to prevent the need to set aside large sections of land for the production of cattle for the cruel practice of slaughter, merely to satisfy mankind's taste for flesh and blood. Such slaughter is a serious form of violence. Anyone can witness the insensitivity and cruelty in the pain and suffering that takes place in slaughterhouses, or in numbing ourselves to be able to kill defenseless creatures to satisfy our tongue without pity or sorrow.

The time for a higher vibration in the world has arrived, if we expect to change the course of history and civilization. The war-like consciousness in humanity must be corrected now or we will miss the chance to upgrade all of society, and we will see quarrel and war continue into our future. It will get increasingly dangerous unless we start taking the violence out of our personal lives by making the proper choices. Otherwise, violence breeds more violence, and the large-scale slaughter of animals is a hideous form of violence and cruelty.

This brutality and mercilessness toward other living beings creates an atmosphere that is extremely detrimental to developing a refined awareness wherein we can recognize the spirit and consciousness of all beings as part of, and a creation from, the Supreme Spirit. If we remain so insensitive and heartless in such a way as to continue animal slaughter and meat consumption, we also continue to be less concerned about each other, and certainly less able to understand or follow the depths of the 11th commandment. We should also bear in mind that any cruelty we do is observed by our own conscience, our own soul, as well as the Supersoul form of God in our heart and in the hearts of all living beings.

Killing animals to eat ignores the consciousness within them, and causes our unnecessary participation in the pain and suffering of other beings. Injury and torment deliberately done to other creatures, no matter how small, will cause the plight of continued pain and suffering for those who commit the deed. How can it be otherwise? This breaks the 11th commandment, which implicates all those involved in such acts in darkness. They distance themselves from recognizing the Divine in all beings, and, thus, also from the spiritual kingdom. How can one enter the spiritual domain when recognition of the spirit remains unavailable to him while in this world? How can one's eyes hope to see what appears far away in heaven when you cannot even recognize that it is right in front of you or within you? The spiritual kingdom will, thus, remain far away from you. This knowledge is being given to one and all to relieve you of this consequence. To ignore it means to remain without clarity, in a world of darkness. Choose your world carefully.

God is situated in every one of us. All living beings are intimately connected with God in this way. We should also be aware that the animals and plants are living entities that are simply wearing different bodies. Even animals have a basic consciousness not unlike that of more developed beings. They also struggle to survive and try to avoid suffering and pain. Animals also know how to take care of their young, even if the parent must come in harm's way to protect them. As spirit souls dressed in different forms, they also are all parts and parcels of God. So there must be proper respect for such beings. Though they cannot express their thoughts and feelings so easily to us, they are still exhibiting consciousness and life, which is the symptom of the soul within. That soul is no different than your own soul, but only dressed in a different body that is less developed intellectually.

How can there be a soul in all species? The symptom of the soul is consciousness. If consciousness is there, then a soul is present. What is the difference between a live person and a dead person? The dead lack consciousness, which means the absence of the soul. In the same way with an animal, what is the difference between a live dog and a dead dog? Any animal that shows life exhibits consciousness, which is due to the presence of a soul. What is the difference between the bodies of a human and dog? They are made from the same ingredients, the same elements. When the dog is alive, the consciousness is there. In that case, it also tries to avoid pain, it gets hungry and needs food, it appreciates being loved and petted, and it exhibits its affection by licking your face, which is not so dissimilar to the motivations of human beings.

Even a cow also has consciousness and feelings. Have you noticed how tears flow from a cow's eyes when its calf is taken away? Is this merely some chemical reaction in the brain? This is comparable to the emotions that people display in similar circumstances. That is because consciousness is there, which is the symptom of a soul. This is merely one example of how we can perceive the spirit in all beings, which are part of the Supreme Spirit. If our awareness is open and developed, we can understand that the animal may feel something similar to us when we lose our child. If our sensitivity is shut down, then in our base level of thinking we may conclude that animals like cows are unable to have such feelings, and, thus, we disconnect ourselves from them. We may also think that they feel no pain when it comes time to slaughter them for the pleasure of tasting their flesh. This act itself habituates our insensitivity and inability to evolve and grow spiritually since we remain incapable of perceiving the soul within the body of such an animal or any other being.

Take the example of the chimpanzees that learn how to communicate through sign language. They have shown that they have a high level of reasoning capability, and express likes and dislikes, as well as pain or happiness, and even sadness, grief, and fear. Thus, they have feelings just as we do. They are not merely dumb and insensitive animals to be caged and treated cruelly in any way we want, as many people who lack higher awareness would prefer to think. To do so only shows our inability to evolve to a level of really following and understanding this 11th commandment. Without that development, our spiritual progress remains stunted.

Plants also have consciousness, however limited it may be. This can be seen in how outdoor bushes and shrubs always grow toward the sun as a means for survival. Or, it can be seen in the way experiments have shown wild fluctuations in polygraph machines when one is hooked to a plant and a leaf is cut or burnt, or how a different reaction is seen when it is given water. Thus, even plants have levels of sensitivity that show the presence of consciousness, which again is the symptom of the soul within. Behind all life is spirit.

Animals, however, do not deal in right and wrong. They only act in the way nature has directed them to act, and this is called instinct. In nature and in the animal world, the basic principle is that the strong live off the weak. However, in human society we are expected to be more than that. People can make the choice to act like animals or humans. We should not act in ways that dehumanize ourselves. Human life is one of responsibility to move into higher consciousness. If we do not focus on this endeavor, then one remains in a brutish mentality, acting as little more than a polished animal. How can you raise your consciousness to see the Divine in every living being if instead you are looking at some beings as if they would be appetizing for dinner? That is an animal's view. No one will become very aware of God with this mentality, regardless of how pious they portray themselves to be.

We often see children that are much more sensitive about harming animals and other people. Yet, through the indifference they acquire from adults, they also learn to become more hardened and dehumanized as they grow. They often become more cynical and harsh toward one another as well. Therefore, their chance for higher consciousness and refined awareness becomes unlikely the more they remain in the grips of a callous society.

In this way, the general consciousness of humanity becomes primitive, brutish, and less developed. This also tends to pave the way for an increasingly less tolerant society and one that cares less than they should for the well-being of each other. Because of this, society also must endure the rise in the criminal mentality and even war between men. We must be aware of the various implications of our choices, even our diet. One is always held accountable for the choices and actions one performs, especially when knowledge of right and wrong is persistently given for the benefit of society. Remaining ignorant of the law is no excuse for what befalls humanity in the future.

Of course, there may be times of extraordinary situations or hardship in which one may have to eat whatever is available in order to survive. Then one may be forced to live on the flesh of animals. But one should do this in the mood of thankfulness to those animals who must give up their lives for someone's survival. However, this should not mean that such a standard becomes normal or encouraged. Animals may eat other animals, but we should be more developed than that. A person who does not see the difference certainly does not see the spirit of God in all beings. His vision is covered by a haggard and callous mentality. This is what needs to be corrected.

A point of consideration is that everything comes from God, so even vulnerable creatures are part of the Lord. There is little difference between small children in our own house and defenseless animals. Like our children, the beings within the bodies of unintelligent animals are also as sons and daughters of the Supreme Being. Those whose faculty of judgment is impaired by their own ignorance cannot understand this. Thus, they generally consider only other humans as being worthy of their sympathy. However, God is the Supreme Father of all life, so those who have attained the great recognition of this fact respect all life, and take care not to unnecessarily harm any form of life. There is always a reason why a living being has been placed in a particular type of body, and that is to work out certain desires or experiences. It is not our business to become an impediment in that entity's development if we can avoid it. Treating animals kindly also helps us to develop a refined consciousness that is reflected in the way we treat our fellow human beings. By recognizing the Divinity in all forms of life, we indeed become closer to God.

As all life is precious, we must hold dear all conscious beings and work to accomplish the highest welfare for everyone. We should feel that "I must help others because I am the one who needs the help. I help myself by assisting others. Thus, I look at all beings with a positive attitude, knowing they are the key to my own advancement." The more we provide care and concern for all beings, the more the whole planet feels the affect. Thus, the more we bring about our own progress.

CHAPTER FIFTEEN

Environmentalism According to the 11ᵗʰ Commandment

The environment means nature, and whose nature is it? It is God's nature. Did anyone else create it? Did anyone else put it all together so that it operates the way it does? In fact, mankind is still trying to figure out all the intricacies of how it functions.

In all the inventions or devices we produce, all the ingredients and resources that we use are all given by God through the forces of nature. The elements we need to make big buildings, bridges, ships, cars, or the fuel to operate them, are all being given by God, and we need to show the proper respect. To think we are the proprietors of everything is the illusion. It is our pride that makes us think we are so intelligent, when actually the very brain with which we think is not created by us, but has been given by God.

As everything is created from the Supreme Creator, then we should certainly have a high regard for everything as the expansion of God's energies. This not only includes all of our fellow men, but all creatures, as well as all aspects of the planet. Violence toward the planet in the form of not caring for the environment, misusing and polluting our natural resources, not managing the land and forests properly, are all forms of disrespect toward God and the blessings that have been given us. Why should we expect God to continue giving us the necessities of life, or the means to acquire them, if we are going to ruin them, or do not know how to care for them properly? So we must never pollute our resources or waste the food we have.

We should also see that even the Earth is a living being, full of life. The globe is a mother to us since she supplies all that we need. All of our food, water, and resources for sustaining our own lives, as well as supplies for shelter and clothing, all come from her. How she reciprocates with us in regard to what she provides depends on how we treat, honor, and care for her. The imbalance in nature, such as the greenhouse effect, the changing climate and weather patterns, are reflections of the imbalance in the consciousness of humanity. Once there is balance and harmony in society's consciousness and the way we regard and treat the eco system, this will then be reflected in the balance in the environment. Then many of the storms, along with natural upheavals and disasters will begin to cease.

The environment and the material creation are supplied with the potencies to produce all the necessities that we require, not only for humans but for all species. Human society should not consider itself as the only enjoyer of all of God's creation, and that no other creatures have a claim to it. Humanity is actually a minority species when we consider the many types of creatures that are sustained by the environment. If we manage the ecosystem properly, it will continue to produce everything we need. However, if people who have no genuine spiritual understanding start exploiting the Earth to take whatever they want in any way they want, then the supply of resources will decrease, and the Earth, being a living organism, will stop producing or responding to the needs of society as abundantly as it used to do. Then there will be shortages, droughts, climate collapse, storms, and other difficulties, such as lack of rain and forest fires. Subsequently, the prices on commodities will increase. Gradually more people will become poor, and poverty and starvation will spread in parts of the world. Then we will see fierce competition for whatever resources can be attained. When many people die while fighting over land, water, and other commodities, or over temporary and ever-changing political stances, then all the bloodshed from the dead, dying, or wounded is like offering Mother Earth blood sacrifices to drink. She is pained by this, as are so many other higher beings that watch the activities of humanity. Rather than respecting the Earth and cooperating to share her resources, when we fight over them, it is most heartrending for Mother Earth. Thus, when the

Earth and the Lord's environment are not properly appreciated and maintained, or are exploited by ungodly people, then scarcities and excess pollution is the result. However, nature itself can go on nicely, except for the interference of ungodly men.

As a society controlled by godless men gathers all the resources from the land as fast as possible for power and quick profits, it may appear to be a mighty economic gain at first, but in time it is never enough. As demand grows, scarcity raises its angry head. When the environment is not respected and cared for properly, there are also changes in the various species that have existed for thousands of years, even extinctions. These are all signs of further unknown changes that will be revealing themselves to us when it will be too late.

There may be times when the Earth needs to cleanse herself of unwanted activities or from the pain she suffers from society's wrong aims of life. She may move in various ways to adjust things so that humanity is not so out of balance and to force it to reconfigure its value systems toward the real goal of life. When Earth reacts in particular ways to relieve her from the weight of unwanted activities or segments of society, we should not miss the message. A society that is too spoiled often easily forgets the real reason why we are here.

The proper vision is that everything is the property of the Supreme Being. If we have any possessions or wealth, we should see that we are only borrowing them for a short time. We certainly cannot take them with us when we leave this body at the time of death. Thus, someone else will take it all when we are gone. The ultimate owner of everything is the Supreme Creator. Thus, the proper way to use anything is in the service or consciousness of God. The same goes for taking care of the environment. Everything belongs to God, so, ultimately, we should take care of it as if we were being watched by God and only taking care of His property while, by God's good graces, it produces the resources we need to live. After all, as the Lord in our heart and as the Supersoul of every living being, He is observing everything we do.

All of one's land, home, wealth, and possessions belong to the Supreme Being though we wrongly think, "I am this body and all that belongs to it is mine." Thus, a person of wisdom should not see anything as separate from the Supreme Lord. In spiritual consciousness, such a person will see everything, whether it be fire, air, water, the Earth, the sun and stars, all living beings, the trees and plants, the rivers and oceans, and, in fact, everything that exists as an expansion of the energies of the Supreme Lord. Even while actively engaged with so many objects and undertakings in this creation, a person who sees the whole world as the energy of the Supreme Being is indeed a great sage of wisdom.

Therefore, we should care for the environment as if it is not ours but God's property, and in this way assure ourselves that it will continue to provide all of our necessities for many years to come, and into many future generations.

CHAPTER SIXTEEN

Being Aware of Reactions to Our Activities and Intentions

Whether it is our diet, the way we treat each other, or the way we view other living beings, or how we preserve the environment, everything we do now will produce reactions which affect our future, both individually and socially. Just as the state of the world today, whether good or bad or a combination of such, has been affected by our social development in the past, what we do today will also bring results that will be felt in the future. Thus, in many ways our situation is given to us by our past deeds. On a social level, when a civilization is godless, nature itself produces reactions to that godlessness and exploitative consciousness. A godless society cannot help but conduct itself in a way that gradually deteriorates its own well-being both now and into the future. Though they may have numerous so-called intellectuals and committees and plan-making sessions, they cannot perceive the harm they are doing to themselves, and the dangers that are approaching just over the horizon. This is especially the case if it gets in the way of the profits they are determined to make, even at the expense of the future of the planet.

In this way, we can see that the sufferings of human society are due to the polluted aim of life, which is the origination of all pollution. When people are too materialistic, they forget the real spiritual goal of existence. Thus, they run after sense pleasure with little understanding and little regard for the results of their own foolish acts. Only later must they contend with the reactions that befall them, leaving them in a sorry or distressed state. Because of this pattern, the distress of the world intensifies rather than diminishes.

It is primarily unnecessary wants and desires that push a person into the extra complications of life. These are the cause of confusion, suffering, and discontent that a person feels in the mind. This takes away the happiness that one could attain through a simple way of life. This is why we need to pursue the spiritual lifestyle based on the 11th commandment and cultivate contentment with what easily can be attained with minimal endeavor. We need to discriminate between what is eternal and that which exists only in the temporary field of sensual activity. As it is said, a wise man does not put much emphasis on temporary pleasures or achievements, knowing full well that they all have a beginning and end. The end of all such happiness and pleasure opens the door to various kinds of disappointment, stress, and misery. Thus, we must develop renunciation and detachment from that which is ephemeral and fleeting, and remain free from such unwanted weights and attachments to our consciousness and life.

Real freedom is freedom from unnecessary and unwanted desires. These usually burden us with the endeavors that take time and energy to acquire those things that often do very little good for us. When we become free from such desires and the attempts to satisfy them, then real contentment and self-satisfaction has the chance to shine forth from the heart. Then our future also becomes all the more positive and illuminating.

As spiritual beings, no one dies, but we only change our material identity or costume. Consciousness goes on even after it separates from the body. The life one experiences after this will be but a reflection of one's actions and choices made during the course of this life. Thus, by following this 11th commandment and making just and true choices based on the implications of this code of conduct, one cannot help but progress forward to happier and brighter realms of existence, both in this life and the next. This commandment is given to you for that purpose. So choose well in this life, which is of short duration compared to what is possible for you in the next.

CHAPTER SEVENTEEN

Being a Reflection of God's Unconditional Love

In the deeper levels of understanding the 11th commandment, it means to attain love of God and exhibit that love toward all of His parts and parcels, such as all people, all beings, and all creation. We can do this by knowing and seeing their connection with God as spiritual beings and as His energy. It is to realize that God's love for all of us is available as a constant factor. All we need to do is to plug into that love and allow that love to flow through us. If we are going to be any kind of representative of God's love, a vehicle through which God's love can be experienced, we must know how to be a reflection of God's unconditional love.

In considering how to be a reflection of God's unconditional love toward all beings, we must try to see all beings as God would see us. This means to recognize that deep within the body lays the soul. The soul is free from faulty characteristics or conditions. Being a part and parcel of God, the soul is pure in its essential form. It desires and imagines only what it ought to desire. It is only the mind, body, and intellect that participate and motivate us in sensual desires and bodily actions. We only need to regain and uncover that spiritual identity of ours to awaken our natural spiritual position and awareness. By doing this, we can again awaken our spiritually loving disposition and become free from the faults that keep us motivated toward bodily perceptions and desires. We must realize our own spiritual relationship with God and with all others.

The basic propensity for the living entity is to love. No one lives a life without loving someone. Every living being has this tendency because it is the natural condition of the soul. Even an animal will have a general loving nature toward its young. The missing point is where to direct our love. In our materialistic conception of life, we often direct our love toward an object or person that has a temporary identity. We may love our wife or husband or children or parents, but they all have a temporary existence. Plus, our love for them is usually based on their temporary bodily identity in relation to our own. When that identity changes or they die, we become disappointed or forlorn over the loss. However, when our relations are based on spiritual truth, which is the divine knowledge of the soul, then there can be some aspect of eternality to it, depending on the depth of spirituality to which we take it. The more deeply we base our relations and our love for each other on the divine knowledge of the soul, the more realistic it becomes. Then when we base our love on that truth, and when we direct our natural loving propensity toward God, and we see how all of us are extensions of Him and His loving potency, then we can be truly happy and complete.

The next step is to know that God always loves all of his sons and daughters, especially those who are sincerely trying to approach Him on the spiritual path. Since we are spiritual parts of God, our natural position is also to be loving and caring toward others. The more we are spiritually awakened, the more that natural loving propensity is also awakened. Our own soul becomes fulfilled by rekindling that loving attitude, and God, being the Soul of all souls, seeing that loving disposition in us, is satisfied to see such a wise person being a friend to everyone.

The Lord is pleased when we greet others with tolerance, kindness, friendship, and equality. This means that a person of wisdom will greet everyone in such a way, recognizing the spiritual similarities we all share that are far beyond whatever differences there may be in the types of bodies we have. He or she is also tolerant toward those that may act unkindly due to a lack of spiritual understanding. Those without spiritual perception may have little respect for others, or look upon some as inferior merely due to bodily conditions or circumstances. A person of wisdom treats them with tolerance and kindness in order to set an example of how to act, and also to try to help that person advance spiritually. However, if a person of wisdom comes in contact with someone who is too envious and offensive, such a person should be left alone and avoided, thus preventing him from becoming more abrasive. He may have his own issues to work out and may only become more agitated and disturbed if we try to get him to see the logic in utilizing spiritual knowledge in his life. One should also tolerate whatever insults may occur and never fail to show proper respect to anyone. Avoiding identification with your material body, you should not create enmity with anyone. If you meet someone who is too insulting or abusive, then simply walk away, wish the person well, and pray for his change and growth.

Furthermore, a person of wisdom should always be compassionate to the poor, and respectful toward those who are elevated with spiritual knowledge. A wise person, free from envy because of understanding the spiritual position of everyone, prays for the welfare and advancement of all living beings.

Those who are not merciful to other living beings cannot reach the spiritual domain. Only those persons of wisdom who engage in, or support, welfare activities for other living entities can reach the spiritual strata. This is the importance and further indication of the 11th commandment.

You must try to become purified in heart and consciousness so God can manifest in you and through you. Deep within ourselves, as spiritual beings, we are situated in pure goodness. This only needs to be revealed and reawakened. This is the true nature within us all. We are all beings of light. This is revealed once we are freed from the darkness of ego, which now may be covering us.

Regaining our position here on this Earth as beings of light means we can change this planet into a world of light. Now, what kind of world do you prefer? Would you choose a world of increasing darkness, divisions, and confusion, or a world of harmony, cooperation, light, and love? The answer should be obvious, which means that the next step in social development must also be clear.

Therefore, when you become a reflection of God's love, it is no longer merely a consideration of what you can do that may make a difference, but it is what God does through you. That will become your power, the power of spiritual love that causes miracles to happen. These miracles will happen to you and through you as a being of light, and is symptomatic of one in tune with God.

Everything is ultimately based on truth, and this spiritual truth is synonymous with love. This love is the need of the soul in its search for its natural environment, which is the basis of ultimate spiritual reality. The purpose of human life is to elevate our consciousness to perceive the spiritual strata and to live on that plane of existence. This dimension is full of unbridled, spiritual loving relations. Therein, the need of the soul to express its loving propensity can be fulfilled without limit. Everyone can be truly happy through this process and by attaining this level of reality. This, ultimately, is what we are all seeking. As we become increasingly spiritualized in our consciousness and awareness in this earthly realm, we need to reflect that love toward others as much as we need and long for receiving it.

We must remember that this planet is God's world, but its condition is up to us. God has given us the instructions and knowledge to know what to do, and the Supreme has also given us the free will so we can decide for ourselves what kind of future we want to have for this world. But for the best future possible, we must lead a truthful, noble, and spiritual life. We should not think of ourselves all the time, but we must remember those who are needy and in distress and suffering. We must think of how we can help those who have miserable lives, who have no peace or happiness, or insufficient food.

We must develop universal love in our hearts. To achieve this, we must perform the spiritual practice that purifies our consciousness in a way that develops our perception of the Divine in all living beings. We have a responsibility toward this world, and that is love and the endeavor to spread the spiritual knowledge which allows others to reach this perception. Through universal love we will see the Divine in all beings, and by actually seeing all beings as parts of the Divine, we cannot help but love everyone. Then we will know true inner peace, equanimity, and contentment. That is what leads the way to the kind of joy that we are all seeking.

We have to rise to the level of loving every creature, no matter how great or small. We have to rise to what a real human is meant to be, and that is a person of wisdom whose consciousness can perceive the Divine in all living entities, for every being is a manifestation or spark of the Supreme consciousness.

God's love is unconditional, free to everyone like the sunshine. The sun does not limit where its light goes. It does not shine only on certain countries or particular people. It shines on everyone, everywhere. Similarly, God's love is everywhere for everyone. It may only seem like we are far away from God. This is due to our lack of spiritual perception and a contrary or negative mindset or disposition. This is another form of materialism that is really a cause for what may appear to be our separation from the spiritual strata. Such a mindset has to be corrected, and we do this by acknowledging our inability to advance without God's grace.

As we humble ourselves before God, and we approach God through prayer and service, then our doubts, confusion, and difficulties can and will begin to disappear. It is the reciprocation between God and ourselves that makes all the difference. We will feel this connection more deeply as our own realization of this relationship develops. As this perception grows, we can begin to gain clarity and understanding of our true spiritual position.

It's like taking a shower. We may be ever so dirty and unclean, but if we stay in the shower long enough and follow the procedure of washing ourselves, we will eventually get clean. In the same way, if we stay on the path of service to God and humanity, and follow the method for raising our consciousness, we will gain clarity and spiritual vision. Everything will become clear. Then we will also see how God is everywhere, in everything, and for everyone. We will see through the meaning of this 11th commandment. We will see how we are all parts of the Divine. We will understand how God has never forsaken us or abandoned us. God has only waited for us to turn toward Him. God has only given us the time and the choice as to when we will come to our senses, our spiritual senses. It is never too late.

When we gain our spiritual senses, we can then see Divinity in everything, whether seemingly good or bad. The sun is like the reflection of the inner light of the soul. The more spiritual we become, the more purified our consciousness becomes, and the more aligned we are with the Supreme consciousness. Then the more the light of our own soul will brighten our own sphere of influence with whomever we come in contact. And the more we change the world in a truly uplifting way. As an increasing number of people enter that realm of true, genuine, and nonsectarian spiritual development, the more we bring in a new potential, possibility, and positive future to this planet.

In this way, we can change the course of the world and bring it from darkness to light. God has given this choice to us. It is up to us to create the world as we want it and as it should be. We simply have to use the spiritual knowledge that God has given us. Remember, the state of the world is only a reflection of the general mass consciousness of the people who inhabit it.

So, as we see the environment changing, the climate collapsing, the natural resources that we need dwindling, and pollution spreading, there is only one cause, and that is the misguided aim of society. This is what needs to be adjusted by the advancement of spiritual perception among us.

We can hardly live balanced lives when the eco system of the planet is out of balance. We can hardly expect to be healthy when the environment itself is becoming increasingly unhealthy.

Therefore, we have to reach levels of spiritual realization that are beyond mere rules and regulations and dogmas. They have to be actualized and applied in our everyday lives. In other words, we have to practically see this spiritual reality and then live according to these spiritual realizations on every level. This is the actualization and real impact of this 11th commandment. It must not be viewed as a mere idea or thought, but a level of genuine perception that is applied in all our actions and plans, in every aspect in the way we deal with things. The more any portion of society becomes truly developed spiritually, the more easily civilization as a whole can change in a positive way.

When you see the spiritual unity among all beings, how we are all parts of the Divine, and when you make your own connection with God, then you will be able to truly pray for universal peace and for the welfare of all beings. Unconditional compassion for others is that state in which we can become a vehicle through which God's love can flow through all of us and be felt by all those around us. Then you will also experience a higher consciousness and inner spiritual bliss, contentment, and tranquility. That is the source of the real happiness for which we all seek while in this material creation. It is available to all of us if we only utilize the proper directions. We must always search for our real spiritual identity, and upon realizing it always rest in that perception in all circumstances.

In this way, a true person of wisdom represents the Lord's love for all and is a reflection of that love. Through such an outlook, he or she draws the Lord close because the Lord is pleased by such love. This is the method by which the Infinite becomes submissive to the infinitesimal. Such a person will also feel the reciprocation of the Lord as the Lord's love flows through that person toward all others, and all others who feel that love of God also become more attracted to God. Thus, as this spreads from one person to another, the spiritual dimension increasingly manifests on Earth, and one's soul and one's mission in life becomes completely fulfilled.

CHAPTER EIGHTEEN

Manifesting God's Plan for Humanity and the World

The whole purpose of the material creation is to provide the facilities to allow humanity and all beings to work out their material desires, live a peaceful life, and finally to raise their consciousness to the degree that they can toward attaining the spiritual frequency. In this way, one can enter into the spiritual domain at the time of death as one would enter the real or occupational world after graduating from school.

A person may have to go through so many lessons in this process, some difficult and others easy, and some lessons may not be clearly understood until much later. All of it is meant to help shape the mind and consciousness to a higher level of character and insight, and a clearer degree of receptivity to the purpose that God has for you, and for humanity at large. Many of us have forgotten this purpose, and the need to perceive our real spiritual identity beyond the body. Because of this forgetfulness, we enter so many avenues or struggles in life in order to find happiness. But until we really know who and what we are, we will remain unclear as to what we should really do with our life. We may have many things to work out before we are actually receptive to hear and understand who we are and what truly is our best interest. Nonetheless, the Lord provides this creation for the living beings to attain every experience imaginable within the framework of this material existence, if that is what the entity wants. Until the living being realizes that there is a higher purpose behind it all and becomes inquisitive about it, then he still remains immersed in material consciousness. With the realization of a higher purpose, everything begins to change for him.

To fulfill this purpose, the Lord also supplies various kinds of spiritual knowledge to people in all kinds of places. When a person begins to be receptive to the higher purpose of life, the Lord arranges that he or she will be introduced to the knowledge that is most suitable for his or her progress.

You must always have hope that change and growth will come to you, as well as to society and everyone in the world. There are innumerable beautiful souls that wish for this and are looking for it. Only a small portion of people start trouble, being possessed of a divisive mentality. The few selfish troublemakers spoil it for the many, and may make life difficult for the whole society. But the majority is looking for peace and development of various kinds. They must learn to never give up and to be strong in their means to attain it and stand up for it.

In this way, there is a great need for selflessness, along with the attainment and use of divine wisdom, and the practice that gives genuine and deep spiritual realizations. You must also pick your association carefully and not be with those who are negative and divisive. Be with those who are positive, pleasant, and interested in spiritual development. Then you can gain momentum, encouragement, and strength, and help one another move forward and advance together to higher levels of consciousness and spiritual perception.

We must work to make ourselves whole both individually and collectively by utilizing spiritual knowledge. We must cooperate to manifest the natural spiritual unity that exists between us all. If a new and more progressive world begins to increasingly focus on those most uplifting philosophies, then the religions and views that still hold the blindness to such spiritual unity will become antiquated and even viewed as retarded. Those people who hold onto such a backward consciousness will be left behind and gradually die off. The world will then shed those who wish to keep antagonism, division, and hatred as their philosophy or religion.

A deeper recognition of all beings as rays of light descending from the Supreme is what is needed now, and what is expected of you. Do not disappoint those who are watching you, those lofty beings who are trying to help and guide you. Do not continue to drag this world in the muck of materialism and the darkness of spiritual ignorance. It is time for a change, time for a spiritual revolution. Freedom is at hand, but only if you want it. First you must know what it is and how to acquire it. And this 11th commandment is the next step forward. You must adopt this willingly and progress forward, or the world may never reach its full potential, and the true plan for humanity will be delayed, if not lost for a time.

Genuine persons of wisdom are concerned to put an end to the sufferings and wanderings of the living beings that go through various highs and lows of material existence. The wise may have gone through many such experiences themselves and wish to help end the prolongation of the search for happiness that others may be forced to pursue. So they are willing to share the deep spiritual knowledge they have learned for the benefit of others.

If you think life appears meaningless and overwhelming, then you need to be more focused on a genuine spiritual path. You need to raise yourself a little higher. Someone who is truly on the spiritual path easily overcomes these kinds of problems and knows that all such difficulties are but temporary illusions. In the end truth prevails, but we have to be on the path of truth, the path of spiritual development. Such progress is beyond mere religious determination or sectarian allegiance. We must go beyond those ideologies that divide us. A religion that drives a wedge between us is not real religion, for it needs to rise to the level of genuine spirituality, for that is what can unite us. History has shown that the cause of numerous wars has been religion. Conventional religions often divide, while real spirituality unites. The spirituality that provides the means to see through the superficial bodily distinctions and differences, that reveals the ultimate unity we all share on the spiritual platform, which uncovers the essence of our real identity as the soul, is what is needed and is the mission of human existence. This is the way to rise above the turmoil caused by the confusion of not knowing who and what we really are and what we are meant to do. Now we must decide whether we want to be united and live in peace, or remain divided and forever in conflict and war.

To attain unity we must all sit under the tree of divine spiritual wisdom and insight. It is that tree which emits this 11th commandment. It is under that tree where we all can live in cooperation and love. It is that tree that provides inspiration and spiritual knowledge, and which can burn out the seeds of anger and desire by which goodness, compassion, and equanimity can grow in the heart. The more we work on this individually, the more it will also manifest collectively throughout society.

In order to help usher in such a change on the planet, to manifest God's plan, you must simply find a service to do to assist in its manifestation. Find a way to spend time immersed in spiritual consciousness, in thoughts of God and service to the Supreme, and the means to give that to others. This would be in any way you can serve God and humanity, and spread genuine welfare and spiritual advancement for all beings. This will always have a positive affect for you and those around you.

A wise sage knows that though he may be living peacefully and contentedly in life with his own spiritual realizations, he can still not neglect others. When there is a calamity in society and suffering continues because of challenges, confusion, or a lack of understanding, such sages cannot remain impartial. They must come forward to help bring awareness of our deeper spiritual similarities and, thus, help create a united front that can assist in manifesting God's plan for the world. As people increasingly reawaken their genuine spiritual consciousness, the more God's plan for humanity can manifest in society.

CHAPTER NINETEEN

Social Change to Manifest a New Paradigm

The 11th commandment also means to invoke the necessary positive changes in social consciousness which could indeed bring about a new paradigm. This development will start with the way we view each other, which must be brought to a spiritual standard. The world is in a critical condition wherein change of consciousness must be attained if there is to be progress in the global situation, including politics, international relations, environmental conditions, economics, and inter-religious understanding and respect. It is also critical in the fact that there have been few times in history in which society can accomplish this on such a mass scale, especially in the way we have such facility now for widespread communication, and for quickly and easily distributing information.

All material things exhibit a pattern of having; 1) a beginning, 2) then growth, 3) maintenance, 4) production of by-products, 5) followed by dwindling, and 6) death. All global changes and ideas for improvements will go through these basic stages of life unless there is a spiritual and, thus, a permanent or stable foundation to them. Otherwise, there may be many suggestions that appeal to one's intellect but will ultimately produce nothing more than the six changes mentioned above and what we have already experienced over the course of the last few thousand years in the way of confusion, trouble, conflict, and war. To change the world starts with a difference within ourselves, and in the way we view each other as spiritual beings, as parts of God.

You must recognize that the inner self of your neighbor is the same as your own inner self. They are separate, but no different in spiritual quality. In this sense they are one. One must help the other grow. The actions of one will directly or indirectly affect the other, and, thus, all our actions affect the whole world to some degree. Helping our neighbors serves the good of our own selves, which serves the good of the whole planet. We are all connected in this way, and one's own growth will also accelerate the progress and development of others. Thus, the world may be set free, may be liberated, and may become happy through the process of genuine spiritual knowledge, insight, compassion, true nonviolence, and, most importantly, by enlightenment.

Different areas of the planet and various parts of the greater human family must work together like the various parts of the body. The arms, legs, brain, etc., all work cooperatively so the body can function effectively. All the physical parts of the body work to feed the stomach, and, thus, by the digestion and distribution of nutrients through the stomach, they all have strength and happiness. The absence of such cooperation leads to weakness and suffering for the whole body. Without working together in this way for the common goal of feeding the stomach, then all the parts of the body lose strength and soon can no longer do their service to the body. In such a state, the body gradually shuts down and dies. They cannot be happy on their own or in working alone without cooperation with the rest of the body. The same goes for society.

Therefore, when there is a lack of mutual collaboration amongst humanity, quarrel erupts. This may be between families, or in communities, or in international relations. Then people begin to lose happiness and suffer. Cooperation is imperative if we want a healthy body, family, society, or country. Assisting each other and working together in this world is necessary if we want happiness in this life.

In the end, spiritual truth prevails because that is all that is eternal. It is only the ignorance of mankind that brings forth a dark day of war or terror in global relations on this planet. We all must work together to bring forth such truth again, which is beyond the short-lived relative truths of the distinctions of the body, culture, race, or religion. These differences are all temporary. What is temporary is not truth, but it is only relative. Relative truth is that which may exist, but is in a constant state of change. Thus, it never lasts for long. You must look higher for what is permanent or eternal. That is where you will find real spiritual truth. You, as your real identity, are a part of that eternal truth.

The communication one finds with God, or the linking of the soul with the Supreme Soul, is ultimately the most important thing one can attain in life. The more we all help each other accomplish that, the easier it becomes. Assisting one another on this path, not by force but by genuine spiritual love, is a very high regard to have for one another.

This is the path of love for God, and love for each other, as creations of God. Not that we pride ourselves as being better or superior than another person, or criticize those we think are not good enough, but that we work together to uplift each other. This is the Godly life. This is what God recognizes.

One thing we must bear in mind is that the foundation of this cosmic creation is based on compassion for all living beings. If we are going to be united with the purpose of this creation, then we have to have compassion as one of our prime characteristics. The universe is created to give all beings the chance for expression in a way that can be fulfilling and to encourage them to discover their real potential and higher identity as spiritual beings. Once they become established in the spiritual environment, they no longer need to experience the lower realms of existence within this three-dimensional world. They become free of the limitations that exist therein. The more people rise to the spiritual perception, the more the whole world will automatically change. The more that every human being begins to see through the realization as expressed in this 11th commandment, the more the world will change, reflect, and manifest the spiritual energy and vibration that pervades this creation. Now it has become somewhat hidden because the general mass of people have forgotten it or lost interest, but the more we awaken to it, the more it will again manifest its divinely positive effects on us and this world. It is up to us to take the next step to make the change.

The point is that there is no scarcity in this world for food, water, resources, etc. There is enough to provide for the needs of everyone. Something that may be scarce in one part of the world may be plentiful in another area. But there is a scarcity of spiritual consciousness that would make way for harmony, cooperation, and unity in society. This is what is needed in order to manage and share the resources so that all people have what they need. This alone would change the world in many progressive and necessary ways. It is of prime importance that world leaders attain this understanding and view. If they do not, then as people progress spiritually, it may be the leaders themselves who hinder and delay the positive changes that could manifest in this world as they play their games for profit or domination, and use the general masses as pawns in their schemes. Therefore, such leaders would have to be removed. But people must know the characteristics of one who is a real leader and elect such a person.

Do not be afraid to rise up and make a stand for higher spiritual awareness. We all will have to make a stand at some point if we are going to leave any kind of mark for the benefit of society. We just need to know what is the greatest good.

The more people attain the great recognition of the similarities that we all share between us on the spiritual level, the more likely we can all live as one big family, united in our purpose as spiritual beings. Those who attain the great recognition will be the ones to most effectively change the world. Those who attain the great realization will be the ones to show the way.

Even a small number of truly enlightened souls can guide the rest of humanity through the labyrinth of this existence, toward peace and happiness in this life and the next, not by blind faith or dogma, but by naturally awakening the realization and perception of one's real spiritual identity and the purpose of life. By taking this 11th commandment to heart and working to raise our consciousness to higher degrees of awareness, we can certainly bring about a new paradigm on this planet for increased harmony, cooperation, and peace.

CHAPTER TWENTY

Open Up to the Great Life Within

This 11th commandment as presented herein also means that we should enter the great spiritual life within. People unnecessarily try to move to a place in this world that seems to be the most suitable for them. They are always trying to find happiness by arranging their life and home in a particular way, through external adjustments that they feel will be the most beneficial for their mind, senses, and ego. They think that as soon as they attain a certain facility, status, comfort level, or location, then everything will be fine and they will be happy. Naturally, there may be certain conditions that heighten one's sense of happiness from an external, sensual, or mental point of view. But people often overlook the contentment and joy that comes from within by adjusting one's own consciousness rather than emphasizing one's surroundings or condition.

The initial pollution in the world begins with the contamination of consciousness, which manifests as the false aims of life. These are based on the goal of making the mind and senses happy by mere bodily and sensual activities or arrangements. Essentially, this is lust, which is the selfish interest in one's own pleasure, position, power, and influence. Lust is a master that is never satisfied, nor is the servant of such a master. A society whose goal is based on serving lust becomes increasingly dissatisfied and restless until they practically create a hell on Earth. Then everyone suffers, and the happiness they seek is but a dim reflection of their true potential and the bliss that lies on the other side of the doorway within. This doorway leads to raising the consciousness to spiritual perception, or what we call the great realization, which was described earlier. The path to this door can purify one from the false aims of life and free one from the pollution or trouble that such misdirected ambitions produce in society. The great realization is awaiting you. The more people who can travel through that doorway, or who are trying to do so, the more the kingdom of heaven or the spiritual vibration that is all around us will become apparent and manifest here on Earth.

Once the perception of the great realization is aroused within us, the overall consciousness of humanity will begin to change. This is the precursor for all other necessary changes needed to improve things in the world. It is automatic. The one will follow the other as it spreads throughout society.

Life is meant for being happy. But real happiness, which exists on the spiritual platform, is always steady and, in fact, continually increasing according to one's spiritual advancement. Such persons who understand their spiritual identity, and are satisfied in the self or soul and content within, find happiness everywhere. Those who have realized their real self and also see the Supreme Being residing within their heart and in the heart of all beings, to them belongs eternal happiness and peace. If you want a happier life, a happier family, or a happier country, we need this inner development in order to find such real contentment. Without that, there can be no peace, and without peace there can be no happiness, individually or socially.

The body or one's situation never limits the living being's ability to realize one's spiritual identity. The only limiting factor is the living entity's consciousness or lack of spiritual awareness. When the living entity finally regains his original spiritual consciousness, realizing he is not the body, he naturally feels very happy and jolly, being freed from the limited and temporary perspective one has while being controlled by the illusory, material energy. This is mostly a perceptual problem. Such a person also understands that this material world is not his real home, and it has nothing substantial to offer him since real pleasure and happiness actually come from within on the spiritual level. This is the importance and effect of opening oneself to the great life within, or the spiritual path. Thus, he does not put much emphasis on the conditions in which he finds himself, but places more importance on maintaining contact with the spiritual dimension.

Without spirituality there is little purpose in human life. Otherwise, we would be nothing more than polished animals with little or no difference between ourselves and the creatures in the jungles that do what they want with no restraints. Even now we can see some humans that are more cruel and ferocious than animals. We can also see that as society becomes less and less spiritually inclined, the more selfish, heartless, and cruel people become. In this way, without genuine spirituality, the opportunity of human life becomes wasted, like killing one's own soul. Thus, we must never take this human existence nor the opportunity for spirituality for granted.

Following a spiritual path that can actually provide the means to perceive our higher self is one of the most unique adventures life has to offer. On this quest one can understand that there is a divine order to things--everything is happening for a reason. What may be reversals in life now may be only preparations for better things yet to come, which may not manifest unless you were to experience whatever trials are presently happening. They are like tests through which one passes to attain a better level of understanding. When you look at life as a spiritual unfolding, then everything in life has a reason, a purpose. That purpose is for your ultimate good, your greatest development. Or, it is to help you find your full potential, at least if you do not miss the message. In that light, no matter what happens, you are always getting better, wiser, higher, and closer to who and what you really are meant to be.

We must understand that pain and suffering exist only within the illusion of worldly life. It does not exist in the spiritual dimension. Therefore, why do we keep putting ourselves, along with our attention and focus, in to the midst of worldly consciousness, in the illusion? Why do we keep making the same mistakes and suffering the same pains from the illusory existence when we can attain real happiness, peace, tranquility, and contentment on the path toward the spiritual domain? This should be our real goal of life.

So, let us change our life as needed to make the attainment of spiritual perception our main goal. Let us realize that materialistic life will never give us the true joy and bliss that we all seek. Such being the case, let us adjust our lives so that we work in the world only as much as necessary, and then focus ourselves on the higher purpose of life. When this is our goal, then our destiny becomes wonderful.

In our ordinary affairs we must be strong and firm. Life requires great courage and strength. But we must not use the goal of spirituality as an excuse to neglect our duties to family and occupation. However, do not take on too much for yourself. Do not let things become an over-endeavor. Only do whatever you can, or your work will become a source of stress and will oppress you with unnecessary anxiety and worry. Understand your own limitations in this regard and work within those boundaries. Stay focused on what matters most and do it well, both materially and spiritually. The more spiritual you become, the more easily you will be able to face the challenges of life. Inner transformations will take place in you that will change your perception and respect for life. Then you can be a friend to everyone.

With peace in your heart you will not speak badly or abusively about others or to them. You will not hurt others with your thoughts, words, or deeds. Then people will seek you out for your positivism, good energy, and wisdom. Fill your heart with love and peace and let it radiate throughout the universe.

Every living being is destined to ultimately reach the Supreme Lord at some point. Everyone at some time will be able to understand his or her relationship with God if they are sincere. How long this may take is up to each person. It depends on how deep you go into it. But every person has this hidden treasure, a destiny with God that everyone should seek. When one finds this treasure or even gets a glimpse of it while on the path, such a person becomes perpetually rich or spiritually complete. This is the great treasure within, and the profound inner life one can attain. God is waiting for you to see it. Troubles in society that are due mostly to the false and external goals of life often leave one feeling empty, inadequately satisfied, unfulfilled, or still trying to fill the hole within. But these will not so easily disturb one when such a person regains his or her spiritual perception and real identity. This is the importance and the potential that a person can attain by opening up to the great life within--the spiritual consciousness beyond all material limitations. The doorway is waiting for you to go through it. All philosophies, religions, spiritual paths and instructions, methods of contemplation or meditation, and the many challenges in life, are all meant to be an impetus to lead people to this door. That is the goal, the awakening of who you really are. This opportunity is now before you. Do not let it slip away.

CONCLUSION

Giving the 11th Commandment to Others

If we are going to see to it that a new paradigm of social spiritual development continues, not only for others here and now but also for future generations, we must make sure that we attain and live by a higher set of values that is based not merely on theory or faith alone, but on a superior spiritual perception that is actualized and awakened within us. This must be based on our spiritual identity that is beyond all the ordinary bodily distinctions, such as race, color, nationality, etc. that are often the basis of how we see and relate to each other.

If we expect to ever change this world to one that is truly civilized and progressive, both outwardly and inwardly, then we must all reach an elevated level of recognizing that we are more than these physical machines or bodies in which we reside. After all, who does not think that a change for improvement is overdue? This is not in regard to technological development, but the enhancement of our consciousness which is what determines how and in what direction we use our scientific achievements. Otherwise, without such a change, we are only giving our children the same narrow view of how to relate with each other, and the same limited potential for carrying on into the future. In such a case, this will only escalate the discontent, envy, suspicion, hatred, and wars that envelope so much of the world. This 11th commandment is here to change that, if people can only understand and follow it seriously.

We also need to make sure that we are not merely sheep in a flock that follows a leader without question. We must see to it that we can attain our own spiritual realizations that are more than just the dictates of a religious dogma that actually makes us prisoners of religion. We need to make sure we are not merely passing along to the next generation rules of a religion that were meant for control and manipulation, or stifling our means to fully question things. Or that were for establishing power over the masses by policing or reducing our own spiritual growth and potential, rather than giving freedom to investigate and explore the higher realms of consciousness through which we can understand who we really are. Personal realizations are the only way that growth and change can be genuine. Merely following the instructions of others is not the way for real social growth and advancement, or the implementation of a new spiritual perception, although lessons from those who are spiritually advanced is, indeed, the way we begin the path. If we are not humble enough to take instruction from others, then we will never be qualified to reach the stage of perceiving the higher, spiritual reality.

For this reason, we must also make sure that religious leaders are in fact real leaders, qualified by their own spiritual lifestyle and able to give a higher consciousness to others, or at least guide people so they can attain it themselves. Such teachers must not be fakes who hide their bad habits behind closed doors while posing as pure and righteous, or as if they have some special communication with God while nursing all the lusty desires or fanatical attitudes that any common man has. Such a leader is merely a pretender. He may have some charisma but will lack spiritual potency and authenticity for inspiring real change and growth.

We must have a leader who is capable of throwing out those elements that thrive on division and separatism, which can become the seeds for quarrel and war. We must make way for genuine moral and spiritual development. If a leader, whether political or religious, cannot do that, then he or she is hardly someone who can take people to the proper level of a truly civilized society that has regard for all beings.

We need to be guided by a person who can break down the barriers of superficial perception and show us that we are all friends, all beings who share this planet and share the future that we make for it. We share in the results of the efforts to create harmony, cooperation, and unity by our willingness to recognize our similarities rather than our differences, and by our willingness to assist in each other's growth.

A true spiritual path unites us, it does not divide us. It frees society to the potential of attaining their own insights and realizations of their higher identity and possibilities, and the spiritual similarities they share with all others. It frees them from their past conditionings and opens them to new realms of achievement and the dawn of new beginnings. It frees them to live according to their own realizations rather than to the conditioned responses they may have been trained to repeat. It frees them to experience boundless bliss, and rise above the limitations that are considered normal in the bodily or physical realm. It also frees them from the fear of death, knowing it is but a door to so much more, beyond time, beyond suffering, if our lives are used positively.

We can indeed create a brighter future by focusing our thoughts and consciousness on our spiritual identity as outlined in this 11th commandment. This may be difficult for some people at first, because of egoistic attachments to a material identity, which is often perpetuated by the network of news media, advertisements, and politics. The more we remain in the grip of such a mentality, the less opportunity we have to give others, including our own children, the freedom from the same self-inflicted constraints and limited view of who we are. We can and must do better than that, not only for ourselves but also for the future generations of this world.

However, the more we remain focused on this spiritual awareness and view of ourselves and all others, as outlined by this 11th commandment, the more we can remain outside the snare of selfish limitations through the freedom provided by genuine spirituality. This brings a person to a position and perspective beyond all shortcomings and trappings of ego and image. The more we work on this together, giving and reminding each other of the logic of the 11th commandment, the more we will see beyond such differences as race, body color, nationality, culture, religion, sex, etc. Then the more easily we develop and work in a world of cooperation, consideration, compassion, and harmony. The more we work in this way, the brighter we become, the more positive our attitude is, and the more we create an increasingly uplifting future for ourselves and the world. If there is a cause to stand for, then this is it.

We also must be thankful that through genuine spirituality we have a continuous opportunity to discover who we are as spiritual beings and live according to that identity. That is what can bring the most positive exchange between ourselves and all others, and lift us up from the constraints of our materialistic conception of who we are and the superficial differences between us. It is this deeper spirituality that can evaporate our apparent dissimilarities and raise us up to see how we are all connected and share the same spiritual characteristics. This vision alone is one that can bring joy and comfort. That is the opportunity and the blessings that are found within the instructions of this 11th commandment, and which makes it worth giving to others for their upliftment, nonsectarian spiritual development, and inner harmony and peace. The more people who can be assisted in this way, and who can understand and follow this commandment, the more there is the opportunity for bringing about a positive future for this world. This is why it is so important as the next step for social spiritual development.

INDEX

11th commandment............. 7
    basis of Spiritual Truth 49
    new code for guidance 11
    part of Universal Spiritual
        Truths 20
    reason for it 5
Addictions........................ 65
Asanas
    promotes better health 144
Attachment
    to our material form 13
Bad habits......................... 65
Being spiritual 144
Blessings of God 80
Bodily externals 14
Brotherhood of humanity.. 47
Children of God 50
Civilizations 71
Compassion
    for all living beings ... 113
    genuine concern for
        others..................... 51
Competition 81
Contentment.............. 66, 99
Crime.............................. 72
Criminals
    flourish due to impotent
        heads of state......... 72
Death 29
    does not give automatic
        enlightenment........ 84
Diet.................................. 88
Divine
    in all living beings....... 35

Duty of God to humanity 6
Duty of humanity
    take this knowledge
        seriously 6
Eating animals................. 88
Economic development..... 79
Economics........................ 77
Ego 30
Environmentalism............. 94
False ego
    attachment to what is
        unreal.................... 30
False self
    ego-based image of
        ourselves 58
Freedom 99
Fulfillment........................ 8
God
    has a purpose for each of
        us........................... 42
    reciprocates with us..... 33
    situated in all beings.... 90
    Supreme Father of life. 93
    we are all reflections of 45
Godless society
    gradually deteriorates .. 98
Gods unconditional love . 100
Great realization 7, 15, 34, 115
    perceiving God in all
        beings 17
Great recognition......... 15, 38
    all beings same in
        spiritual quality 47
    we are all son and

daughters of the same
Supreme Father 42
Happiness 116
Harmony
when it can manifest ... 13
Hatred
enemy of the 11th
commandment 83
Hatred, jealousy and pride
destroyers of our future 60
Human life
one of responsibility 92
Hunger problems
solving 88
Illusion 46
Industry 79
Inner Self 111
Leaders 114
Leadership 70
Mantra-yoga
especially for this age 147
Material body
like a foreign dress 58
Material energy
always changing 53
Materialism
cannot provide complete
fulfillment 8
Miscreants
flourish due to
incompetent heads of
state 72
Modern technology 63
Mother Earth 95
Natural resources 75, 79
New paradigm 111
Nonviolence 83

Pain and suffering
exist only in the illusion
of life 117
Peace 116
in your heart 118
Peace and happiness 66
People must hear the Truth . 6
Person of wisdom 54
Plan of God 12
Politicians 70
Politics 70
Polluted aim of life 98
Pollution
begins with
contamination of
consciousness 115
original source of it 13
Positivism
can spread 51
Proper leadership 75
Prosperity 79
Purpose
of religion 47
Purpose of the material
creation
.... 107
Reactions
to our activities 98
Real happiness 14, 68
Real peace 68
Religion
based on locality deters
real progress 12
must be based on
Universal Spiritual
Truth 8
purpose remains

unfulfilled.............. 47
should show
    attractiveness by
    spiritual purity....... 84
that expands by violence
.... 49
Religious leaders............. 121
Reversals in life.............. 117
Ruler
    should have perfect
        morality................. 75
Self-satisfaction............... 99
Shame........................... 45
Social consciousness....... 111
Soul
    has eternal relationship
        with God............... 28
    in all species.............. 90
    needs for complete
        freedom 65
Souls nature...................... 28
Spirit soul.......................... 55
Spiritual consciousness..... 53
Spiritual dimension
    manifests in one's
        consciousness........ 48
Spiritual energy................ 40
Spiritual identity............... 14
Spiritual life 115
Spiritual loving relationship
    all that can satisfy the
        soul...................... 31
Spiritual path
    its real purpose 41
Spiritual realization
    beyond mere rules and
        regulations........... 105

Spiritual Truth.................... 5
Spirituality
    purpose of human life 117
Spiritually advanced person17
Stress............................... 64
Supersoul.................... 16, 33
    is infinite 28
Supreme Being
    everything is the property
        of.......................... 96
Supreme Lord
    ultimate cause and shelter
.... 39
Taxes............................... 73
Temporary nature
    of all things material ... 57
True spiritual path.......... 122
Unity.............................. 110
Unity and harmony
    why the lack of it........ 13
Universal love 103
Universal Presence............. 4
Universal Spiritual Truths
    are applicable for
        everyone 6
Vibration of energy 36
Violence 83
    justified use of............. 86
    toward the planet......... 94
War and terrorism over
        religion 48
Weapon
    in self-defense............. 86
Yoga
    benefits...................... 144

ABOUT THE AUTHOR

Stephen Knapp grew up in a Christian family, during which time he seriously studied the Bible to understand its teachings. In his late teenage years, however, he sought answers to questions not easily explained in Christian theology. So he began to search through other religions and philosophies from around the world and started to find the answers for which he was looking. He also studied a variety of occult sciences, ancient mythology, mysticism, yoga, and the spiritual teachings of the East. After his first reading of the *Bhagavad-gita*, he felt he had found the last piece of the puzzle he had been putting together through all of his research. Therefore, he continued to study all of the major Vedic texts of India to gain a better understanding of the Vedic science.

It is known amongst all Eastern mystics that anyone, regardless of qualifications, academic or otherwise, who does not engage in the spiritual practices described in the Vedic texts cannot actually enter into understanding the depths of the Vedic spiritual science, nor acquire the realizations that should accompany it. So, rather than pursuing his research in an academic atmosphere at a university, Stephen directly engaged in the spiritual disciplines that have been recommended for hundreds of years. He continued his study of Vedic knowledge and spiritual practice under the guidance of a spiritual master. Through this process, and with the sanction of His Divine Grace A. C. Bhaktivedanta Swami Prabhupada, he became initiated into the genuine and authorized spiritual line of the Brahma-Madhava-Gaudiya *sampradaya*, which is a disciplic succession that descends back through Sri Caitanya Mahaprabhu and Sri Vyasadeva, the compiler of Vedic literature, and further back to Sri Krishna. At that time he was given the spiritual name of Sri Nandanandana dasa. In this way, he has been studying and practicing yoga since 1971, especially bhakti-yoga, and has attained many insights and realizations through this means. Besides being *brahminically* initiated, Stephen has also been to India more than 20 times and traveled extensively throughout the country, visiting most of the major holy places and gaining a wide variety of spiritual experiences that only such places can give. He has also spent nearly 40 years in the management of various Krishna temples.

Stephen has put the culmination of nearly 50 years of continuous research and travel experience into his books in an effort to share it with those who are also looking for spiritual understanding. More books are forthcoming, so stay in touch through his website to find out further developments.

More information about Stephen, his projects, books, free ebooks, and numerous articles and videos can be found on his website at: www.stephen-knapp.com or http://stephenknapp.info or his blog at http://stephenknapp.wordpress.com.

Stephen has continued to write books that include *The Eastern Answers to the Mysteries of Life* series:
1. *The Secret Teachings of the Vedas: The Eastern Answers to the Mysteries of Life*
2. *The Universal Path to Enlightenment*
3. *The Vedic Prophecies: A New Look into the Future*
4. *How the Universe was Created and Our Purpose In It*
   He has also written:
5. *Toward World Peace: Seeing the Unity Between Us All*
6. *Facing Death: Welcoming the Afterlife*
7. *The Key to Real Happiness*
8. *Proof of Vedic Culture's Global Existence*
9. *The Heart of Hinduism: The Eastern Path to Freedom, Enlightenment and Illumination*
10. *The Power of the Dharma: An Introduction to Hinduism and Vedic Culture*
11. *Vedic Culture: The Difference it can Make in Your Life*
12. *Reincarnation & Karma: How They Really Affect Us*
13. *The Eleventh Commandment: The Next Step for Social Spiritual Development*
14. *Seeing Spiritual India: A Guide to Temples, Holy Sites, Festivals and Traditions*
15. *Crimes Against India: And the Need to Protect its Ancient Vedic Tradition*

16. *Yoga and Meditation: Their Real Purpose and How to Get Started*

17. *Avatars, Gods and Goddesses of Vedic Culture: Understanding the Characteristics, Powers and Positions of the Hindu Divinities*

18. *The Soul: Understanding Our Real Identity*

19. *Prayers, Mantras and Gayatris: A Collection for Insights, Protection, Spiritual Growth, and Many Other Blessings*

20. *Krishna Deities and Their Miracles: How the Images of Lord Krishna Interact with Their Devotees*

21. *Defending Vedic Dharma: Tackling the Issues to Make a Difference*

22. *Advancements of the Ancient Vedic Culture*

23. *Spreading Vedic Traditions Through Temples*

24. *The Bhakti-yoga Handbook*

25. *Lord Krishna and His Essential Teachings*

26. *Mysteries of the Ancient Vedic Empire*

27. *Casteism in India*

28. *Ancient History of Vedic Culture*

29. *A Complete Review of Vedic Literature*

30. *Bhakti-Yoga: The Easy Path of Devotional Yoga*

31. *Destined for Infinity*, an exciting novel for those who prefer lighter reading, or learning spiritual knowledge in the context of an action oriented, spiritual adventure.

BOOKS BY STEPHEN KNAPP

If you have enjoyed this book, or if you are serious about finding higher levels of real spiritual Truth, and learning more about the mysteries of India's Vedic culture, then you will also want to get other books written by Stephen Knapp, some of which include:

The Secret Teachings of the Vedas

The Eastern Answers to the Mysteries of Life

This book presents the essence of the ancient Eastern philosophy and summarizes some of the most elevated and important of all spiritual knowledge. This enlightening information is explained in a clear and concise way and is essential for all who want to increase their spiritual understanding, regardless of what their religious background may be. If you are looking for a book to give you an in-depth introduction to the Vedic spiritual knowledge, and to get you started in real spiritual understanding, this is the book!

The topics include: What is your real spiritual identity; the Vedic explanation of the soul; scientific evidence that consciousness is separate from but interacts with the body; the real unity between us all; how to attain the highest happiness and freedom from the cause of suffering; the law of karma and reincarnation; the karma of a nation; where you are really going in life; the real process of progressive evolution; life after death—heaven, hell, or beyond; a description of the spiritual realm; the nature of the Absolute Truth—personal God or impersonal force; recognizing the existence of the Supreme; the reason why we exist at all; and much more. This book provides the answers to questions not found in other religions or philosophies, and condenses information from a wide variety of sources that would take a person years to assemble. It also contains many quotations from the Vedic texts to let the texts speak for themselves, and to show the knowledge the Vedas have held for thousands of years. It also explains the history and origins of the Vedic literature. This book has been called one of the best reviews of Eastern philosophy available.

Trim size 6"x9", 320 pages, ISBN: 0-9617410-1-5, $14.95.

The Vedic Prophecies
A New Look into the Future

The Vedic prophecies take you to the end of time! This is the first book ever to present the unique predictions found in the ancient Vedic texts of India. These prophecies are like no others and will provide you with a very different view of the future and how things fit together in the plan for the universe.

Now you can discover the amazing secrets that are hidden in the oldest spiritual writings on the planet. Find out what they say about the distant future, and what the seers of long ago saw in their visions of the destiny of the world.

This book will reveal predictions of deteriorating social changes and how to avoid them; future droughts and famines; low-class rulers and evil governments; whether there will be another appearance (second coming) of God; and predictions of a new spiritual awareness and how it will spread around the world. You will also learn the answers to such questions as:

- Does the future get worse or better?
- Will there be future world wars or global disasters?
- What lies beyond the predictions of Nostradamus, the Mayan prophecies, or the Biblical apocalypse?
- Are we in the end times? How to recognize them if we are.
- Does the world come to an end? If so, when and how?

Now you can find out what the future holds. The Vedic Prophecies carry an important message and warning for all humanity, which needs to be understood now!

Trim size 6"x9", 325 pages, ISBN:0-9617410-4-X, $20.95.

How the Universe was Created And Our Purpose In It

This book provides answers and details about the process of creation that are not available in any other traditions, religions, or areas of science. It offers the oldest rendition of the creation and presents insights into the spiritual purpose of it and what we are really meant to do here.

Every culture in the world and most religions have their own descriptions of the creation, and ideas about from where we came and what we should do. Unfortunately, these are often short and generalized versions that lack details. Thus, they are often given no better regard than myths. However, there are descriptions that give more elaborate explanations of how the cosmic creation fully manifested which are found in the ancient Vedic *Puranas* of India, some of the oldest spiritual writings on the planet. These descriptions provide the details and answers that other versions leave out. Furthermore, these Vedic descriptions often agree, and sometimes disagree, with the modern scientific theories of creation, and offer some factors that science has yet to consider.

Now, with this book, we can get a clearer understanding of how this universe appears, what is its real purpose, from where we really came, how we fit into the plan for the universe, and if there is a way out of here. Some of the many topics included are:

- Comparisons between other creation legends.
- Detailed descriptions of the dawn of creation and how the material energy developed and caused the formation of the cosmos.
- What is the primary source of the material and spiritual elements.
- Insights into the primal questions of, "Who am I? Why am I here? Where have I come from? What is the purpose of this universe and my life?"
- An alternative description of the evolutionary development of the various forms of life.
- Seeing beyond the temporary nature of the material worlds, and more.

This book will provide some of the most profound insights into these questions and topics. It will also give any theist more information and understanding about how the universe is indeed a creation of God.

This book is 6" x 9" trim size, $19.95, 308 pages, ISBN: 1456460455.

Toward World Peace: Seeing the Unity Between Us All

This book points out the essential reasons why peace in the world and cooperation amongst people, communities, and nations have been so difficult to establish. It also advises the only way real peace and harmony amongst humanity can be achieved.

In order for peace and unity to exist we must first realize what barriers and divisions keep us apart. Only then can we break through those barriers to see the unity that naturally exists between us all. Then, rather than focus on our differences, it is easier to recognize our similarities and common goals. With a common goal established, all of humanity can work together to help each other reach that destiny.

This book is short and to the point. It is a thought provoking book and will provide inspiration for anyone. It is especially useful for those working in politics, religion, interfaith, race relations, the media, the United Nations, teaching, or who have a position of leadership in any capacity. It is also for those of us who simply want to spread the insights needed for bringing greater levels of peace, acceptance, unity, and equality between friends, neighbours, and communities. Such insights include:

- The factors that keep us apart.
- Breaking down cultural distinctions.
- Breaking down the religious differences.
- Seeing through bodily distinctions.
- We are all working to attain the same things.
- Our real identity: The basis for common ground.
- Seeing the Divinity within each of us.
- What we can do to bring unity between everyone we meet.

This book carries an important message and plan of action that we must incorporate into our lives and plans for the future if we intend to ever bring peace and unity between us.

This book is $6.95, 90 pages, 6" x 9" trim size, ISBN: 1452813744.

Facing Death
Welcoming the Afterlife

Many people are afraid of death, or do not know how to prepare for it nor what to expect. So this book is provided to relieve anyone of the fear that often accompanies the thought of death, and to supply a means to more clearly understand the purpose of it and how we can use it to our advantage. It will also help the survivors of the departed souls to better understand what has happened and how to cope with it. Furthermore, it shows that death is not a tragedy, but a natural course of events meant to help us reach our destiny.

This book is easy to read, with soothing and comforting wisdom, along with stories of people who have been with departing souls and what they have experienced. It is written especially for those who have given death little thought beforehand, but now would like to have some preparedness for what may need to be done regarding the many levels of the experience and what might take place during this transition.

To assist you in preparing for your own death, or that of a loved one, you will find guidelines for making one's final days as peaceful and as smooth as possible, both physically and spiritually. Preparing for death can transform your whole outlook in a positive way, if understood properly. Some of the topics in the book include:

- The fear of death and learning to let go.
- The opportunity of death: The portal into the next life.
- This earth and this body are no one's real home, so death is natural.
- Being practical and dealing with the final responsibilities.
- Forgiving yourself and others before you go.
- Being the assistant of one leaving this life.
- Connecting with the person inside the disease.
- Surviving the death of a loved one.
- Stories of being with dying, and an amazing near-death-experience.
- Connecting to the spiritual side of death.
- What happens while leaving the body.
- What difference the consciousness makes during death, and how to attain the best level of awareness to carry you through it, or what death will be like and how to prepare for it, this book will help you.

Retail Price, $13.95, 135 pages, 6"x9" trim size, .

The Key to Real Happiness

This book is actually a guide to one of the prime purposes of life. Naturally everyone wants to be happy. Why else do we keep living and working? Now you can find greater levels of happiness and fulfillment. Using this knowledge from the East, you can get clear advice on the path for reaching an independent and uninterrupted feeling of well-being. This information is sure to open your eyes to higher possibilities. It can awaken you to the natural joy that always exists within your higher Self.

Many people consider happiness as something found with the increase of pleasure and comforts. Others look for position, or ease of living, thrills, or more money and what it can buy. However, by using knowledge from the East and taking an alternative look at what is advised herein, we get guidance on our true position and the means necessary for reaching the happiness for which we always hanker. Some of the topics include:

- What keeps us from being truly happy.
- How all suffering exists only within the illusion.
- Your spiritual Self is beyond all material limitations.
- How to uplift your consciousness.
- How your thoughts and consciousness create your future and determines your state of happiness and outlook on life.
- How to defend yourself from negativity.
- How real independent and self-sufficient happiness is already within you, and how to unveil it.
- How to enjoy that ever-existing pleasure within.
- This book and its easy to understand information will show you how to experience real happiness and joy, and reach the spiritual level, the platform of the soul, beyond the temporary nature of the mind and body.

Retail Price: $6.95, 95 pages, trim size 5 1/2" x 8 1/2", ISBN: 1-930627-04-1.

Destined for Infinity

Deep within the mystical and spiritual practices of India are doors that lead to various levels of both higher and lower planes of existence. Few people from the outside are ever able to enter into the depths of these practices to experience such levels of reality.

This is the story of the mystical adventure of a man, Roman West, who entered deep into the secrets of India where few other Westerners have been able to penetrate. While living with a master in the Himalayan foothills and traveling the mystical path that leads to the Infinite, he witnesses the amazing powers the mystics can achieve and undergoes some of the most unusual experiences of his life. Under the guidance of a master that he meets in the mountains, he gradually develops mystic abilities of his own and attains the sacred vision of the enlightened sages and enters the unfathomable realm of Infinity. However, his peaceful life in the hills comes to an abrupt end when he is unexpectedly forced to confront the powerful forces of darkness that have been unleashed by an evil Tantric priest to kill both Roman and his master. His only chance to defeat the intense forces of darkness depends on whatever spiritual strength he has been able to develop.

This story includes traditions and legends that have existed for hundreds and thousands of years. All of the philosophy, rituals, mystic powers, forms of meditation, and descriptions of the Absolute are authentic and taken from narrations found in many of the sacred books of the East, or gathered by the author from his own experiences in India and information from various sages themselves.

This book will prepare you to perceive the multi-dimensional realities that exist all around us, outside our sense perception. This is a book that will give you many insights into the broad possibilities of our life and purpose in this world.

Published by iUniverse.com, 255 pages, 6" x 9" trim size, $16.95, ISBN: 0-595-33959-X.

Reincarnation and Karma: How They Really Affect Us

Everyone may know a little about reincarnation, but few understand the complexities and how it actually works. Now you can find out how reincarnation and karma really affect us. Herein all of the details are provided on how a person is implicated for better or worse by their own actions. You will understand why particular situations in life happen, and how to make improvements for one's future. You will see why it appears that bad things happen to good people, or even why good things happen to bad people, and what can be done about it.

Other topics include:
- Reincarnation recognized throughout the world
- The most ancient teachings on reincarnation
- Reincarnation in Christianity
- How we transmigrate from one body to another
- Life between lives
- Going to heaven or hell
- The reason for reincarnation
- Free will and choice
- Karma of the nation
- How we determine our own destiny
- What our next life may be like
- Becoming free from all karma and how to prepare to make our next life the best possible.

Combine this with modern research into past life memories and experiences and you will have a complete view of how reincarnation and karma really operate.

Retail Price, $13.95, 135 pages, 6" x 9" trim size.

Vedic Culture
The Difference It Can Make In Your Life

The Vedic culture of India is rooted in Sanatana-dharma, the eternal and universal truths that are beneficial to everyone. It includes many avenues of self-development that an increasing number of people from the West are starting to investigate and use, including:

- Yoga
- Meditation and spiritual practice
- Vedic astrology
- Ayurveda
- Vedic gemology
- Vastu or home arrangement
- Environmental awareness
- Vegetarianism
- Social cooperation and arrangement
- The means for global peace
- And much more

Vedic Culture: The Difference It Can Make In Your Life shows the advantages of the Vedic paths of improvement and self-discovery that you can use in your life to attain higher personal awareness, happiness, and fulfillment. It also provides a new view of what these avenues have to offer from some of the most prominent writers on Vedic culture in the West, who discovered how it has affected and benefited their own lives. They write about what it has done for them and then explain how their particular area of interest can assist others. The noted authors include, David Frawley, Subhash Kak, Chakrapani Ullal, Michael Cremo, Jeffrey Armstrong, Robert Talyor, Howard Beckman, Andy Fraenkel, George Vutetakis, Pratichi Mathur, Dhan Rousse, Arun Naik, Parama Karuna Devi, and Stephen Knapp, all of whom have numerous authored books or articles of their own.

For the benefit of individuals and social progress, the Vedic system is as relevant today as it was in ancient times. Discover why there is a growing renaissance in what the Vedic tradition has to offer in *Vedic Culture*.

Published by iUniverse.com, 300 pages, 6"x 9" trim size, $22.95, ISBN: 0-595-37120-5.

The Power of the Dharma
An Introduction to Hinduism and Vedic Culture

The Power of the Dharma offers you a concise and easy-to-understand overview of the essential principles and customs of Hinduism and the reasons for them. It provides many insights into the depth and value of the timeless wisdom of Vedic spirituality and why the Dharmic path has survived for so many hundreds of years. It reveals why the Dharma is presently enjoying a renaissance of an increasing number of interested people who are exploring its teachings and seeing what its many techniques of Self-discovery have to offer.

Herein you will find:

- Quotes by noteworthy people on the unique qualities of Hinduism
- Essential principles of the Vedic spiritual path
- Particular traits and customs of Hindu worship and explanations of them
- Descriptions of the main Yoga systems
- The significance and legends of the colorful Hindu festivals
- Benefits of Ayurveda, Vastu, Vedic astrology and gemology,
- Important insights of Dharmic life and how to begin.

The Dharmic path can provide you the means for attaining your own spiritual realizations and experiences. In this way it is as relevant today as it was thousands of years ago. This is the power of the Dharma since its universal teachings have something to offer anyone.

Seeing Spiritual India
A Guide to Temples, Holy Sites, Festivals and Traditions

This book is for anyone who wants to know of the many holy sites that you can visit while traveling within India, how to reach them, and what is the history and significance of these most spiritual of sacred sites, temples, and festivals. It also provides a deeper understanding of the mysteries and spiritual traditions of India.

This book includes:

- Descriptions of the temples and their architecture, and what you will see at each place.
- Explanations of holy places of Hindus, Buddhists, Sikhs, Jains, Parsis, and Muslims.
- The spiritual benefits a person acquires by visiting them.
- Convenient itineraries to take to see the most of each area of India, which is divided into East, Central, South, North, West, the Far Northeast, and Nepal.
- Packing list suggestions and how to prepare for your trip, and problems to avoid.
- How to get the best experience you can from your visit to India.
- How the spiritual side of India can positively change you forever.

This book goes beyond the usual descriptions of the typical tourist attractions and opens up the spiritual venue waiting to be revealed for a far deeper experience on every level.

Crimes Against India:
And the Need to Protect its Ancient Vedic Traditions

1000 Years of Attacks Against Hinduism and What to Do about It

India has one of the oldest and most dynamic cultures of the world. Yet, many people do not know of the many attacks, wars, atrocities and sacrifices that Indian people have had to undergo to protect and preserve their country and spiritual tradition over the centuries. Many people also do not know of the many ways in which this profound heritage is being attacked and threatened today, and what we can do about it.

Therefore, some of the topics included are:

- How there is a war against Hinduism and its yoga culture.
- The weaknesses of India that allowed invaders to conquer her.
- Lessons from India's real history that should not be forgotten.
- The atrocities committed by the Muslim invaders, and how they tried to destroy Vedic culture and its many temples, and slaughtered thousands of Indian Hindus.
- How the British viciously exploited India and its people for its resources.
- How the cruelest of all Christian Inquisitions in Goa tortured and killed thousands of Hindus.
- Action plans for preserving and strengthening Vedic India.
- How all Hindus must stand up and be strong for Sanatana-dharma, and promote the cooperation and unity for a Global Vedic Community.

India is a most resilient country, and is presently becoming a great economic power in the world. It also has one of the oldest and dynamic cultures the world has ever known, but few people seem to understand the many trials and difficulties that the country has faced, or the present problems India is still forced to deal with in preserving the culture of the majority Hindus who live in the country. This is described in the real history of the country, which a decreasing number of people seem to recall.

Therefore, this book is to honor the efforts that have been shown by those in the past who fought and worked to protect India and its culture, and to help preserve India as the homeland of a living and dynamic Vedic tradition of Sanatana-dharma (the eternal path of duty and wisdom). This is 370 pages, $24.95, ISBN: 978-1-4401-1158-7.

Yoga and Meditation
Their Real Purpose and How to Get Started

Yoga is a nonsectarian spiritual science that has been practiced and developed over thousands of years. The benefits of yoga are numerous. On the mental level it strengthens concentration, determination, and builds a stronger character that can more easily sustain various tensions in our lives for peace of mind. The assortment of *asanas* or postures also provide stronger health and keeps various diseases in check. They improve physical strength, endurance and flexibility. These are some of the goals of yoga.

Its ultimate purpose is to raise our consciousness to directly perceive the spiritual dimension. Then we can have our own spiritual experiences. The point is that the more spiritual we become, the more we can perceive that which is spiritual. As we develop and grow in this way through yoga, the questions about spiritual life are no longer a mystery to solve, but become a reality to experience. It becomes a practical part of our lives. This book will show you how to do that. Some of the topics include:

*   Benefits of yoga
*   The real purpose of yoga
*   The types of yoga, such as Hatha yoga, Karma yoga, Raja and Astanga yogas, Kundalini yoga, Bhakti yoga, Mudra yoga, Mantra yoga, and others.
*   The Chakras and Koshas
*   Asanas and postures, and the Surya Namaskar
*   Pranayama and breathing techniques for inner changes
*   Deep meditation and how to proceed
*   The methods for using mantras
*   Attaining spiritual enlightenment, and much more

This book is 6"x9" trim size, $17.95, 240 pages, 32 illustration, ISBN: 1451553269.

Avatars, Gods and Goddesses of Vedic Culture

The Characteristics, Powers and Positions of the Hindu Divinities

Understanding the assorted Divinities or gods and goddesses of the Vedic or Hindu pantheon is not so difficult as some people may think when it is presented simply and effectively. And that is what you will find in this book. This will open you to many of the possibilities and potentials of the Vedic tradition, and show how it has been able to cater to and fulfill the spiritual needs and development of so many people since time immemorial. Here you will find there is something for everyone.

This takes you into the heart of the deep, Vedic spiritual knowledge of how to perceive the Absolute Truth, the Supreme and the various powers and agents of the universal creation. This explains the characteristics and nature of the Vedic Divinities and their purposes, powers, and the ways they influence and affect the natural energies of the universe. It also shows how they can assist us and that blessings from them can help our own spiritual and material development and potentialities, depending on what we need.

Some of the Vedic Divinities that will be explained include Lord Krishna, Vishnu, Their main avatars and expansions, along with Brahma, Shiva, Ganesh, Murugan, Surya, Hanuman, as well as the goddesses of Sri Radha, Durga, Sarasvati, Lakshmi, and others. This also presents explanations of their names, attributes, dress, weapons, instruments, the meaning of the Shiva lingam, and some of the legends and stories that are connected with them. This will certainly give you a new insight into the expansive nature of the Vedic tradition.

This book is: $17.95 retail, 230 pages, 11 black & white photos, ISBN: 1453613765, EAN: 9781453613764.

The Soul
Understanding Our Real Identity
The Key to Spiritual Awakening

This book provides a summarization of the most essential spiritual knowledge that will give you the key to spiritual awakening. The descriptions will give you greater insights and a new look at who and what you really are as a spiritual being.

The idea that we are more than merely these material bodies is pervasive. It is established in every religion and spiritual path in this world. However, many religions only hint at the details of this knowledge, but if we look around we will find that practically the deepest and clearest descriptions of the soul and its characteristics are found in the ancient Vedic texts of India.

Herein you will find some of the most insightful spiritual knowledge and wisdom known to mankind. Some of the topics include:

*   How you are more than your body
*   The purpose of life
*   Spiritual ignorance of the soul is the basis of illusion and suffering
*   The path of spiritual realization
*   How the soul is eternal
*   The unbounded nature of the soul
*   What is the Supersoul
*   Attaining direct spiritual perception and experience of our real identity

This book will give you a deeper look into the ancient wisdom of India's Vedic, spiritual culture, and the means to recognize your real identity.

This book is 5 1/2"x8 1/2" trim size, 130 pages, $7.95, ISBN: 1453733833.

Prayers, Mantras and Gayatris
A Collection for Insights, Spiritual Growth, Protection, and Many Other Blessings

Using mantras or prayers can help us do many things, depending on our intention. First of all, it is an ancient method that has been used successfully to raise our consciousness, our attitude, aim of life, and outlook, and prepare ourselves for perceiving higher states of being.

The Sanskrit mantras within this volume offer such things as the knowledge and insights for spiritual progress, including higher perceptions and understandings of the Absolute or God, as well as the sound vibrations for awakening our higher awareness, invoking the positive energies to help us overcome obstacles and oppositions, or to assist in healing our minds and bodies from disease or negativity. They can provide the means for requesting protection on our spiritual path, or from enemies, ghosts, demons, or for receiving many other benefits. In this way, they offer a process for acquiring blessings of all kinds, both material and spiritual. There is something for every need. Some of what you will find includes:

- The most highly recommended mantras for spiritual realization in this age.
- A variety of prayers and gayatris to Krishna, Vishnu and other avatars, Goddess Lakshmi for financial well-being, Shiva, Durga, Ganesh, Devi, Indra, Sarasvati, etc., and Surya the Sun-god, the planets, and for all the days of the week.
- Powerful prayers of spiritual insight in Shiva's Song, along with the Bhaja Govindam by Sri Adi Shankaracharya, the Purusha Sukta, Brahma-samhita, Isha Upanishad, Narayana Suktam, and Hanuman Chalisa.
- Prayers and mantras to Sri Chaitanya and Nityananda.
- Strong prayers for protection from Lord Narasimha. The protective shield from Lord Narayana.
- Lists of the 108 names of Lord Krishna, Radhika, Goddess Devi, Shiva, and Sri Rama.
- The Vishnu-Sahasranama or thousand names of Vishnu, Balarama, Gopala, Radharani, and additional lists of the sacred names of the Vedic Divinities;
- And many other prayers, mantras and stotras for an assortment of blessings and benefits.

This book is 6"x9" trim size, 760 pages, ISBN:1456545906, $31.95.

Advancements of Ancient India's Vedic Culture

The Planet's Earliest Civilization and How it Influenced the World

This book shows how the planet's earliest civilization lead the world in both material and spiritual progress. From the Vedic culture of ancient India thousands of years ago, we find for example the origins of mathematics, especially algebra and geometry, as well as early astronomy and planetary observations, many instances of which can be read in the historical Vedic texts. Medicine in Ayurveda was the first to prescribe herbs for the remedy of disease, surgical instruments for operations, and more.

Other developments that were far superior and ahead of the rest of the world included:

- Writing and language, especially the development of sophisticated Sanskrit;
- Metallurgy and making the best known steel at the time;
- Ship building and global maritime trade;
- Textiles and the dying of fabric for which India was known all over the world;
- Agricultural and botanical achievements;
- Precise Vedic arts in painting, dance and music;
- The educational systems and the most famous of the early universities, like Nalanda and Takshashila;
- The source of individual freedom and fair government, and the character and actions of rulers;
- Military and the earliest of martial arts;
- Along with some of the most intricate, deep and profound of all philosophies and spiritual paths, which became the basis of many religions that followed later around the world.

These and more are the developments that came from India, much of which has been forgotten, but should again be recognized as the heritage of the ancient Indian Vedic tradition that continues to inspire humanity.

This book is 6"x9" trim size, 350 pages, $20.95, ISBN: 1477607897.

The Bhakti-yoga Handbook
A Guide for Beginning the Essentials of Devotional Yoga

This book is a guide for anyone who wants to begin the practice of bhakti-yoga in a practical and effective way. This supplies the information, the principles, the regular activities or *sadhana*, and how to have the right attitude in applying ourselves to attain success on the path of bhakti-yoga, which is uniting with God through love and devotion.

This outlines a general schedule for our daily spiritual activities and a typical morning program as found in most Krishna temples that are centered around devotional yoga. In this way, you will find the explanations on how to begin our day and set our mind, what meditations to do, which spiritual texts are best to study, and how we can make most everything we do as part of bhakti-yoga. All of these can be adjusted in a way that can be practiced and applied by anyone by anyone regardless of whether you are in a temple ashrama or in your own home or apartment.

Such topics include:
* The secret of bhakti-yoga and its potency in this day and age,
* The essential morning practice, the best time for meditation,
* The standard songs and mantras that we can use, as applied in most Krishna temples,
* Understanding the basics of the Vedic spiritual philosophy, such as karma, reincarnation, the Vedic description of the soul, etc.,
* How Vedic culture is still as relevant today as ever,
* Who is Sri Krishna,
* How to chant the Hare Krishna mantra,
* Standards for temple etiquette,
* The nine processes of bhakti-yoga, a variety of activities from which anyone can utilize,
* How to make our career a part of the yoga process,
* How to turn our cooking into bhakti-yoga,
* How to set up a home altar or temple room, depending on what standard you wish to establish,
* How to take care of deities in our home, if we have Them,
* How to perform the basic ceremonies like arati,
* How to take care of the Tulasi plant if you have one,
* And the spiritual results you can expect to attain through this yoga.

All of the basics and effective applications to get started and continue with your practice of bhakti-yoga is supplied so you can progress in a steady way, from beginner to advanced.

This is 278 pages, $14.95, ISBN: 149030228X.

Mysteries of the Ancient Vedic Empire
Recognizing Vedic Contributions to Other Cultures Around the World

The Vedic culture is accepted by numerous scholars as one of the most sophisticated civilizations to appear after the last glacial period of 12,000 years ago. It developed in ancient India, and as the people populated the region, they also expanded and spread into other parts of the planet, taking much of their culture with them.

This book takes us on a journey through history and across many countries as we point out similarities and remnants of the Vedic tradition that remain there to this day. These include forms of art, philosophy, religion, architecture, temples, ways of living, and so on. Such countries include: Nepal, Burma, Cambodia, Thailand, Vietnam, Korea, Malaysia, Indonesia, Sri Lanka, Egypt, Africa, the Middle East, Iraq, Afghanistan, Syria, Central Asia, Greece, Italy, Germany, Russia, Ireland, Scandinavia, the Americas, and more.

This book also explains:

•   How many religions in the world have features that clearly descended from the oldest form of spiritual knowledge and truth as found in Vedic Dharma.

•   How Vedic Dharma is still relevant today and can help establish peace through its timeless spiritual wisdom.

•   It also helps unravel and reveal the true nature of the Vedic civilization, and how and why it infiltrated and contributed to so many areas and cultures of the world.

•   It also shows a mysterious side of history that few others have recognized.

This book will help anyone understand how the advanced nature of the Vedic civilization and its universal spiritual principles fit into the development of so many other cultures and still contributes to the upliftment of society today.

This book is the follow-up of a previous volume called Proof of Vedic Culture's Global Existence, but with completely different information and resources, as well as updates, written in a more academic style, using hundreds of references, quotes and notes to verify all the information that is used.

This book is 460 pages, 6" x 9" trim size, $22.95, ISBN - 10: 1514394855, ISBN - 13: 978-1514394854.

A Complete Review of Vedic Literature
India's Ancient Library of Spiritual Knowledge

The Vedic texts of India provide some of the highest levels of spiritual knowledge known to man. But it is not just one book, it is a complete library that offers explanations of many aspects of spiritual development, and of the Absolute Truth, or God. These also describe the processes by which a person can directly perceive and attain the Supreme and enter the spiritual realm.

This book shows how these many texts fit together, their divisions, the supplements, what information they contain, and their philosophical conclusions. The contents of this book include:

Understanding the Spiritual Truths in Vedic Literature;

If You are New to the Study of Vedic Culture;

The Four Primary Vedas;

The Brahmanas and Aranyakas;

The Upanishads;

The Upa-Vedas and Vedangas;

The Sutras and Supplements;

The Smritis;

The Vedanta and Vedanta-Sutras;

The Itihasas;

A Review of the Puranas;

The Srimad-Bhagavatam;

The Preeminent Nature of the Srimad-Bhagavatam;

Different Paths in the Vedic literature;

The Ultimate Path to the Absolute.

This book is 106 pages, 5 ½"x8 ½", Paperback $5.99, and Kindle Ebook $1.99. ISBN-10: 1547278862.

www.Stephen-Knapp.com
http://stephenknapp.info
http://stephenknapp.wordpress.com

Be sure to visit Stephen's web site. It provides lots of information on many spiritual aspects of Vedic and spiritual philosophy, and Indian culture for both beginners and the scholarly. You will find:

- All the descriptions and contents of Stephen's books, how to order them, and keep up with any new books or articles that he has written.
- Reviews and unsolicited letters from readers who have expressed their appreciation for his books, as well as his website.
- Free online booklets are also available for your use or distribution on meditation, why be a Hindu, how to start yoga, meditation, etc.
- Helpful prayers, mantras, gayatris, and devotional songs.
- Over two hundred enlightening articles that can help answer many questions about life, the process of spiritual development, the basics of the Vedic path, or how to broaden our spiritual awareness. Many of these are emailed among friends or posted on other web sites.
- Over 150 color photos taken by Stephen during his travels through India. There are also descriptions and 40 photos of the huge and amazing Kumbha Mela festival.
- Photographic exhibit of the Vedic influence in the Taj Mahal, questioning whether it was built by Shah Jahan or a pre-existing Vedic building.
- A large list of links to additional websites to help you continue your exploration of Eastern philosophy, or provide more information and news about India, Hinduism, ancient Vedic culture, Vaishnavism, Hare Krishna sites, travel, visas, catalogs for books and paraphernalia, holy places, etc.
- A large resource for vegetarian recipes, information on its benefits, how to get started, ethnic stores, or non-meat ingredients and supplies.
- A large "Krishna Darshan Art Gallery" of photos and prints of Krishna and Vedic divinities. You can also find a large collection of previously unpublished photos of His Divine Grace A. C. Bhaktivedanta Swami.

This site is made as a practical resource for your use and is continually being updated and expanded with more articles, resources, and information. Be sure to check it out.

Made in the USA
Columbia, SC
07 July 2023

19892304R00085